BASEBALL RULES IN PICTURES

G. Jacobs & J. R. McCrory

Revised and Illustrated by Michael Brown

Foreword by Ron Luciano

A Perigee Book

Perigee Books
are published by
The Putnam Publishing Group
200 Madison Avenue
New York, NY 10016

Library of Congress Cataloging-in-Publication Data

Jacobs, A. G. (A. Gertrude)
Baseball rules in pictures / G. Jacobs & J.R. McCrory:
revised and illustrated by Michael Brown with an introduction by Ron Luciano.
p.   cm.
Summary: The rules of baseball presented in text and illustrations.
ISBN 0-399-51597-6
1. Baseball—Rules. [1. Baseball—Rules.] I. McCrory, J. R.
II. Brown, Michael   III. Title.
GV677.J33 1990   89-77992 CIP AC
796.357′02′022—dc20

Printed in the United States of America
1 2 3 4 5 6 7 8 9 10

This book has been printed on acid-free paper.
∞

CONTENTS

FOREWORD

The man, or woman, on the field in charge of a baseball game is called the umpire. Of course, if he makes a questionable call against the home team on a play, he will be called many other things too. I was a major league umpire for eleven years, and I always called the plays as I saw them—when I saw them. Players and managers often questioned my eyesight, my judgment, even my sanity, but they never questioned my knowledge of the rules.

An umpire has to know the rule book. His job depends on it. I found during my career that those players and managers who really knew the rules were able to take full advantage of a situation on the field. I've seen teams lose games because a player left a base earlier than permitted, or because a pitcher didn't realize he was committing a balk. And, in 1914, a team actually lost the pennant because a runner did not know he had to touch second base when the batter hit a single and a runner on third base scored the "winning" run.

The basic rules of baseball are not complicated. Perhaps the simplest explanation of the rules I have ever heard came from the grandmother of a childhood friend of mine. "One man throws the ball at another man," she said. "The other man tries to hit it with a stick. If he is able to hit it, he is so happy that he runs around like a crazy person!"

Actually, she almost had it right. Baseball is a game of throwing, hitting, catching, and running. And once you have mastered those skills, you will be able to play the game on any level. But as important as it is to be able to do those things, you must know the rules of the game.

When I was growing up in Endicott, New York, we had to make rules that conformed to our ball field. If a ball rolled down a water grate the batter was entitled to a double. If a ball went rolling down the hill, the last one down—the last player to get on his knees—had to get it. And finally, if it went anywhere near Biondo's Bakery, the place with the sweetest rolls and most delicious cakes I've ever tasted, I was not allowed to retrieve it.

But as I got older, and baseball fields became a little more uniform, I learned that a single set of rules governs all organized baseball. I liked that—unlike math, a subject in which every time I thought I'd learned it, they would add another rule or complication.

Knowing the rules will not help you hit a pitch farther or enable you to throw a better fastball. What it will do is give you the same opportunity to win as the most knowledgeable player on the field. The player who doesn't know the rules starts with a disadvantage that sometimes even talent isn't enough to overcome.

I think baseball is the most beautiful game there is to watch, and one of the most enjoyable to play. But to play it right, you have to know the game inside and out. So remember, learn the rules, keep your eye on the baseball, and please, please, never, ever argue with the umpire.

He's trying just as hard as you are—and he may be my relative.

Ron Luciano

INTRODUCTION

During the 1986 American League pennant race, an Italian fellow just recently settled in New York phoned his friend, a diehard Mets fan, and asked him out to dinner. "No," said the fan, "but you can come over and watch the game with us if you like." The Italian, we'll call him Dino, happily accepted, but waited until he arrived to ask, "What game?" Patiently, the fan and his other fan friends seated Dino front and center before the television and proceeded to explain the game. The inning ended, the teams switched places, and a batter came to the plate. Suddenly all the explanations came together for Dino. His jaw dropped and he said, horrified, "You mean that one man with the stick must now play against all the others while his team sits??"

* * *

Although some would say that anyone who doesn't like baseball is un-American, the truth probably is that people who don't like baseball generally don't know baseball. This book is designed to help those people and anyone else—baseball players, managers, or fans—who'd like to have a more thorough knowledge of the rules. The pictorial format and simple language should make the rules of baseball clear even to novices. It is not a complete listing of every rule—the entire Official Playing Rules from the *Professional Baseball Rules Book* are listed in the back of the book—but an overview, intended to present the most important aspects of the game. If you'd like to know more about one of the rules we cover, reference numbers to the specific rule are included in brackets.

As anyone knows who has ever tried to plow through the official rule book of any sport, those publications can sometimes leave nonlawyers shaking their heads. Dino had the help of his patient friend; we offer this volume, and hope it will provide a painless introduction for the novice and an entertaining refresher for those with more experience. Knowing the rules will not help players throw the ball harder or more accurately, nor will it raise batting averages. However, if the time spent looking through this book increases your enjoyment of the premier sport of the United States or gives you an advantage on the field that leads to another run or a much-needed out in the ninth, it will have been time well spent.

HISTORY

It has been estimated that baseball is played by a minimum of six million people each year in the United States. It is so popular that many people consider this summertime game our national pastime. If you include the participants from other countries where baseball is popular, such as Cuba, Japan, Taiwan, Canada, Colombia, and Venezuela, the numbers become staggering. And if you count fans, the number probably surpasses a billion. Its popularity is not surprising considering that there is no one physical type or age that predominates in baseball players. Tall, short, heavy, light, young, and old, all can play this game, which is itself a fascinating combination of different athletic skills, psychology, luck, and ability.

Many people cherish the belief that Abner Doubleday invented baseball. This myth has Doubleday's game first being played in 1839 at Cooperstown, New York—now home of the Baseball Hall of Fame. Doubleday later became a general in the United States Army and died at the end of the century. A few years after Doubleday's death, Albert Spaulding, a former player who made sports equipment, organized a commission to determine the origins of baseball. Although most people felt that Doubleday's game was just another version of a game already being played in the 1830s, a letter from a man who claimed to be Doubleday's boyhood friend was enough to convince the commission that the general had indeed "invented" baseball. Albert Spaulding was very wealthy and very determined to prove that baseball was a wholly American invention; there is some doubt about whether his handpicked commission came to an unbiased conclusion.

In truth, as early as 1600 people in England were playing a game called *rounders* that very much resembled modern baseball. The main difference between the games is that in rounders, runners were put out when they were hit by a thrown ball while off base—like the children's game of kickball.

Americans were playing the game well before the Revolution and even calling it, among other things, base-ball. There was no standardized set of rules; every group of players had their own ground rules. General Doubleday's game was no more like modern baseball than hundreds of other versions being played at the time. That began to change sometime before the Civil War, when Alexander Cartwright organized the Knickerbocker Baseball Club in New York and wrote a set of standard rules in 1845. Although still a long way from the game we play today, the sport took on a regularized and recognizable form.

In the game that generally was being played in the mid-nineteenth century, the first team to make twenty-one runs won the game; the idea of nine innings didn't come until later. Batters were out if their batted ball was caught on the fly or the first bounce. The pitcher stood only forty-five feet from the batter (today it's sixty and one-half feet), and there was no such thing as a walk. The good news for batters, though, was that only swung-at balls counted as strikes, and foul balls never counted as strikes.

The Civil War helped spread the game around the United States. Then in 1869 the first professional team, the Cincinnati Red Stockings, was formed. An eight-team National League was established in 1876, and the American League came into existence around the turn of the century. By the 1950s, there was an American or National League team—also know today as the big leagues or majors—in most of the larger cities from coast to coast.

Each league has an eastern and western division; each American division has seven teams, and each National has six, for a total of twenty-six teams. During the season, which stretches from midspring into autumn, each team plays 162 games. At the end of the regular season, the division leaders play a seven-game series to win the pennant, or championship, of their league. Winners then go on to play each other in the World Series, which is won by the team that wins four games first. Fans generally refer to the World Series simply as "the Series." Granted, the tag "world series" is something of a misnomer, since to date teams come solely from cities in the United States and Canada. Given the worldwide popularity of the sport, however, that could well change in the future. But for all practical purposes today, the Series is considered to be the contest for the world championship.

A number of other leagues play in the United States. These are called the minors and serve as a training ground for the big league. There are many minor leagues and well over 100 league teams. The top class in the minors is the Triple A.

And of course there's the Little League for players eight to twelve years old, as well as other youth-oriented programs such as the Babe Ruth League, the Pony League, and the league run by the American Legion. The National Collegiate Athletic Association and National Association of State High School Athletics Associations administer college and high school baseball programs respectively, as well as a host of other nonaffiliated leagues. The rules of most of these leagues differ slightly from the rules in the majors. The variations generally were made to accommodate the needs of the players. For instance, in Little League games the boundaries of the field are reduced; obviously, an eleven-year-old player has slim hope of hitting the ball out of a ballpark the size of Shea Stadium.

Although slight rule differences do exist, all the leagues are playing the same game. To understand the basics of the rules as they are applied in the majors, with just a little further study of your league's particular rules, is to understand the rules of baseball.

HOW THE GAME IS PLAYED

The object of baseball is to score runs. A run is scored each time a batter becomes a base runner and, by moving in a counterclockwise direction, safely touches first, second, third, and home bases. In order to score the run, base runners must touch home plate before the third out of the inning is made against their team. Each run counts as one point. The team with the most runs at the end of the game wins. [1.02]

The offensive team is the one that is batting, running the bases, and trying to score runs. A batter becomes a base runner either by hitting a fair ball or by being awarded a base or bases by the umpire.

The defensive team is the one that has nine players in the field pitching, catching, standing on or near the bases, and generally trying to prevent the batters from becoming runners and the runners from scoring runs. They try to stop runs by putting the batters and runners out. In general, a batter may be put out by striking out or flying out, and a base runner may be put out by being tagged with the ball or by having the base he's running for tagged. After three outs are made, the teams switch roles. The fielders go into the dugout to wait for their turn at bat, and the other team leaves its dugout and takes up positions in the field. [5.07]

Most of the players on the defensive team may be stationed anywhere in fair territory. Only the pitcher and the catcher must start the play from assigned positions. [4.03]

If for some strange reason the manager wanted the players to all stand in a semicircle around the pitcher, they could; but there are very good reasons and a very strong tradition that places each of the players in a certain position. In the infield, these positions are pitcher, catcher, first base, second base, shortstop (between second and third bases), and third base. In the outfield, players are positioned at right field, center field, and left field.

The game is divided into nine innings. A fair percentage of games last only eight and one-half innings, however, since there is no need to play the second half of the last inning if the team that would bat last is already winning. Other games last longer than nine innings because in the case of a tie, extra innings are played until one team has more runs than the other at the end of a complete inning. [4.10] Every season the majors have at least one game that drags on into the thirteenth or fourteenth inning or longer. The longest game on record was set in 1920 when the Boston Braves played twenty-six innings against the then–Brooklyn Dodgers.

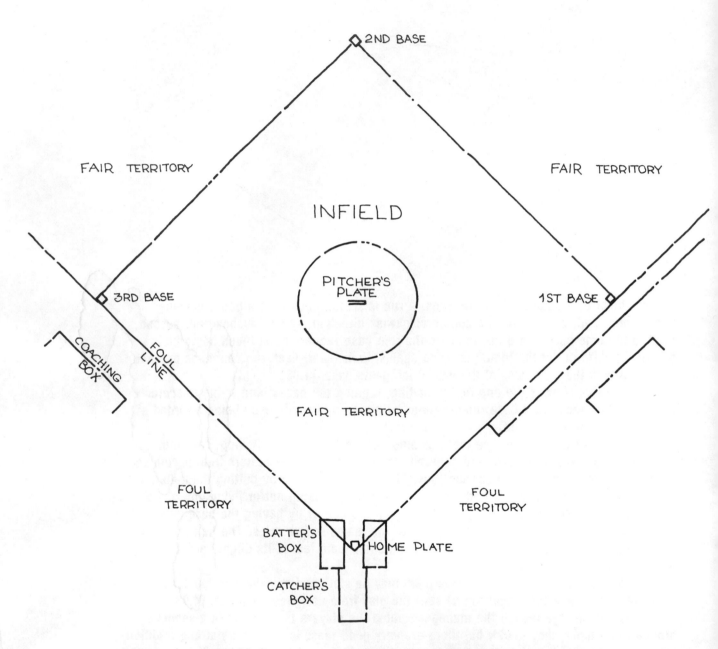

The game is played on a diamond-shaped field with the four bases located at each corner of the diamond. The field is divided into the infield (within the diamond) and the outfield (beyond the diamond). The field is also divided into the fair territory inside the foul lines (see the diagram) and the foul territory outside the lines. The lines themselves are part of the fair territory.

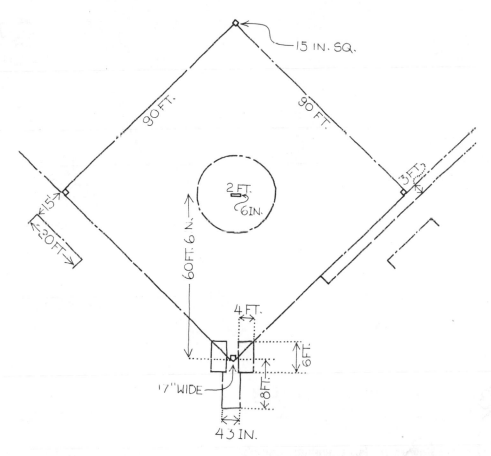

The distance from the outfield fence to home plate varies, but in a modern park it should be at least 325 feet as measured along the foul lines. In older parks the distance may be less. [1.04]

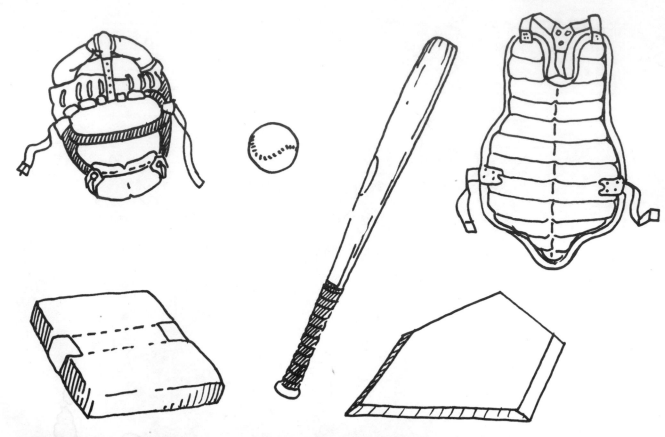

Regulations also govern the size, weight, and shape of the bats, balls, gloves, bases, and other equipment. The regulations covering the bat, for instance, require that the bat be no more than forty-two inches long and two and three-fourths inches in diameter. It must be one piece of solid, round wood. A bat may have tape or pine tar on the gripping surface, but it may not extend any more than eighteen inches from the end of the bat. Grooved or laminated experimental bats are not permitted. [1.10] Other gear is also covered in the rules—for example, the length, sharpness, and shape of the spikes on the players' shoes is regulated. Shoes resembling track shoes (with very sharp spikes) may not be worn. [1.11]

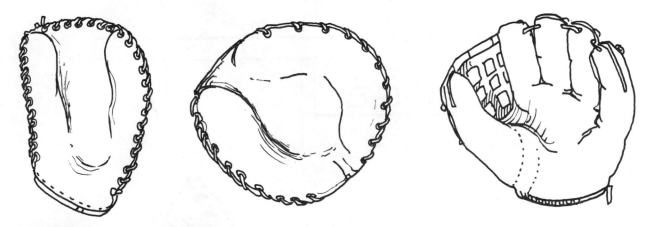

The catcher and the player at first base are the only ones permitted to wear mitts rather than gloves. [1.12, 1.13] Mitts are more padded and mittenlike, with no separations between the fingers, while the gloves have the separations and are lighter, less padded, and more flexible. The catcher and first baseman catch more fast, hard-thrown balls than the other players, so they need the extra protection. There are specific regulations governing the size and shape of mitts and gloves.

All players must wear identically styled uniforms with numbers at least six inches long on their backs. The home team usually wears white. [1.11]

THE PITCHER

The pitcher stands in the center of the diamond and throws the ball for the batters to try to hit. In the early days of baseball—before three strikes and you're out—pitching was more of a courtesy than an athletic feat aimed at making the batter fail. Today, the pitcher's role is so important that in the statistics, a team's win is also counted as a pitcher's win.

The pitcher is allowed eight warm-up pitches at the beginning of each inning. [8.03] There is no batter at the plate while the pitcher takes the warm-ups. The umpire will call ''play ball.'' When the pitcher takes a legal position and the catcher is in the catcher's box, the pitcher will be considered ready to pitch. [5.02]

The pitcher must follow a number of rules in order to be pitching properly. Without these rules, batters would have much too hard a job getting hits and base runners would hardly ever be able to steal, resulting in a much less interesting game. When the pitcher ignores the pitching regulations, an illegal pitch or a balk will be called. [8.04, 8.05]

Some General Rules for Pitchers

If no runners are on base to distract the pitcher with base-stealing attempts, the pitcher must pitch the ball within twenty seconds of receiving it. [8.04] The catcher also must return it promptly to him. The penalty for delaying the game will be a ''ball'' for the batter. If an intentional delay is repeated, the pitcher is ejected.

The pitcher may not intentionally pitch at the batter. A ball that is thrown at the batter is known as a bean ball. Umpires may either warn pitchers that they could be ejected from the game, or simply eject the pitcher on the spot for throwing a bean ball. If the ump believes the throw was the manager's idea, the ump may eject the manager also. [8.02]

The pitcher may not deface the ball in any way and should not throw a shine ball, spit ball, mud ball, sandpaper ball, ear wax ball, mighty bubble-bubble gum ball, or Dr. Hiram P. McGillicutty's baldness-tonic-and-liver-potion ball. The first offense will give the hitter a ''ball''; a second offense penalty will be ejection from the game. [8.02]

The pitcher may use one of two starting positions, the ''set position'' or the ''windup position.'' Either is legal at any time.

THE WINDUP POSITION

In the windup position, the pitcher must stand squarely facing the batter. One foot—called the pivot foot—must be on or on and in front of the pitcher's plate. (The pitcher's plate is a rectangle of rubber in the center of the pitcher's mound.) The other foot is free but must not be lifted from the ground except to throw the ball. The actual throwing motion may include one step forward and one step backward with the free foot, but not more than one in each case. [8.01]

THE SET POSITION

In the set position, the pitcher "faces" the batter sideways with the entire pivot foot in contact with the pitching plate—either on it or partially in front of it. The pivot foot may not be off the end of the pitching plate, which is often called the rubber. From the set position the pitcher may "stretch" but must come to a complete stop before pitching. [8.01]

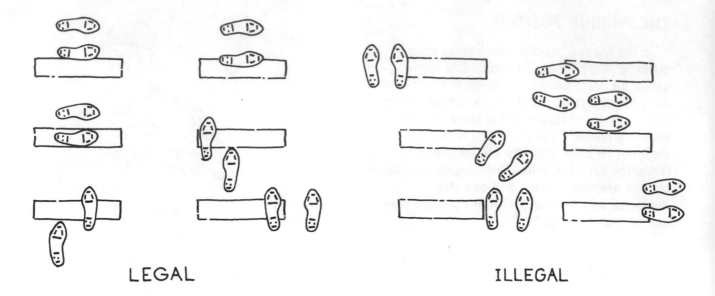

LEGAL   ILLEGAL

From these positions, the pitcher must either

- pitch to the batter;
- step off the rubber and drop hands to the sides;
- or throw to base to try to catch a runner taking a lead. [8.01]

A pitcher who decides to throw to a base must step off the rubber and step directly toward the base to which the ball will be thrown.

Balks

The penalty for an illegal pitch is that the umpire will call a "ball" for the batter. [8.01] However, if runners are on base when the illegal pitch is made, it's called a balk. A "ball" is not called; instead, all the runners—but not the batter—are awarded an advance of one base. [5.09] If there has been a balk pitch and the batter manages, on a hit or otherwise, to advance to first and all the other runners advance, the play will stand. The point of the balk rules is to keep the pitcher from having an unfair advantage by feinting pitches and throws. [8.05]

Some of the many ways for a pitcher to balk are:

- faking a pitch to the batter, then throwing to base to catch the runner; [8.05]
- faking—but not completing—a throw to first base (the pitcher may bluff to second or third; that isn't a balk); [8.05]
- making any motion normally associated with the pitch and then not completing the pitch; [8.05]
- throwing to any base to catch a runner without stepping toward that base; [8.05]

- taking up a position on or near the rubber without possessing the ball; [8.05]
- and dropping the ball, even accidentally. [8.05]

A manager or coach may visit the pitcher on the mound only once during an inning. A second visit means the pitcher is headed for the showers—that is, being replaced by another pitcher. [8.06]

Pitchers and substitute pitchers must complete pitching to at least one batter (or until the side is retired) before they can be replaced—unless they are injured. They can, however, be switched in the middle of pitching to a subsequent batter; for instance, while there's a batter up with one strike and two balls, the manager can change the pitchers. [3.05]

The Designated Hitter

The biggest difference between the American and National leagues is the designated hitter rule. In the National League, every player who plays a position on the field must bat, including the pitcher. In the American League, a batter may be picked to hit and run the bases for the current pitcher or for any other pitchers who later enter the game. This batter is called the designated hitter and must be listed on the lineup card before the game. The rationale behind the designated hitter rule is that the pitcher, who works very hard during the game, may be too tired to hit well; hitting is the most difficult skill in the game. The fresh player batting in place of the pitcher provides for a little more excitement in the game. The designated hitter rule was not intended to make the substitution and resubstitution of players an extremely complicated maneuver. To prevent any confusion from arising, the designated hitter is locked into the batting order and may not take up a defensive position during the game. If the manager does assign the designated hitter a defensive role, then there no longer is a designated hitter and the pitcher must bat in place of the replaced fielder. The designated hitter may be replaced by a pinch hitter who will then take his place in the batting order. This new player is now the designated hitter. A replaced designated hitter may not re-enter the game for any reason. [6.10]

In general, substitutions—one player is removed from the game, and another takes his place—may be made any time the ball is dead. (More on dead balls later.) The batting order stays the same; the substitute player simply takes the place of the replaced player. A player removed from the game cannot return to the game; this explains why there is often applause when a player is removed—the team plays on, but this player's performance is over. [3.03]

THE BATTER

The batters must come promptly, in an established order, to take their turns at bat. The first batter in each inning is the player who is next in order after the last batter of the previous inning. [6.01, 6.02]

When one player is at bat, the next player in the batting order is said to be "on deck." When at bat, hitters must wear a hard batting helmet. [1.16] When the action begins, the batter should stand with both feet inside one of the batter's boxes, which are outlined areas to the left and right of home plate.

The batter's feet may touch the batter's box lines or even be partially outside them; that's still considered to be within the box. [6.03]

Once the pitcher is set and the batter is in the ready position, the pitcher throws the ball past the batter, more or less over home plate, for the batter to try to hit. The batter may decide to swing at the pitch or not. [5.03]

It is the umpire behind home who calls the pitches. The two most frequent calls are "ball" and "strike." Three strikes and the batter is out and must return to the bench or dugout. [6.05, 3.17] There are a number of reasons a strike may be called, the main ones being:

• Strike! The batter swings at a pitched ball and misses it. If the ball hits the batter it doesn't matter; the batter swung so it's a strike. If the batter starts to swing, then decides not to, the umpire will try to judge whether the batter has moved the bat halfway through the swing over home plate or not. The umpire will often ask the advice of the first- or third-base umpire for this call. [2.00]

• **Strike! Some part of the pitched ball passes through some part of the strike zone and the batter doesn't try to hit it. The strike zone is the area over home plate that begins at the top of the batter's knees and ends halfway between the waist and the shoulders when the batter is in a natural, bat-swinging position. [2.00]**

• Strike! The batter hits the pitch foul; that is, the ball settles outside the foul lines. The important exception here is that this kind of strike can only be called for the batter's first and second strikes, not the third. The only time a foul hit can be called as the third strike is when it was a bunt. [2.00] (To attempt a bunt, the batter deliberately strikes the ball lightly without an actual swing of the bat. The ball rolls slowly along the base line, forcing a defensive player to leave his position and rush forward for the ball.)

Less common reasons to call a strike include:

- if a pitch touches the batter in the strike zone; [2.00]
- if the batter touches the ball while swinging at it; [2.00]
- or if the batter is hit by his or her own batted ball while in the batter's box. [2.00]

If the ball is fouled straight back to the catcher, who catches it, it is not a fly ball and the batter is not out. This is called a foul tip. However, if a foul tip is caught when the batter already has two strikes, it does count as the third strike and the batter is out. [2.00]

A batter may not leave the position in the batter's box after the pitcher comes to a set position or starts the windup. Even in the batter's absence from the plate, when the pitch comes it will be called a strike or a ball, as the case may be. [6.02]

Balls

If the umpire calls four balls, the batter will be awarded first base without danger of being put out. [6.08] Called balls prevent the pitcher from pitching only bad, unhittable pitches to good batters, and make it more difficult to trick good runners into trying to steal bases and then catch them out. A ball will be called if:

- a pitch is not swung at and does not enter the strike zone;
- the not-swung-at pitch hits home plate or the ground before entering the strike zone; [2.00]
- the pitcher makes an illegal pitch while the bases are unoccupied; (If the bases are occupied it's a balk.) [8.01]
- or the batter is hit by a ball pitched outside the strike zone, and the batter did not try to avoid it. (The ball is "dead" and runners may not advance.) [6.08]

WHEN THE BATTER IS OUT

The two most common ways a batter may be put out are (1) the batter hits a fair or foul fly ball and the catcher or a fielder catches it [6.05]; (2) three strikes are called. (There's an exception to this when the catcher drops or fails to catch the *third* strike—more about this later.) (p.41) [6.06]

A catch means that the fielder must hold the ball that was in flight long enough to prove to the officials that a secure hold was achieved on the ball in the hand or glove. It may ricochet off another player—for instance, in a case where two fielders are scrambling for a catch—or be juggled before being caught, but it may not ricochet off an object and then be caught. It's not a catch if the player catches the ball after it ricochets off a base runner or an umpire, or if the player drops it because of falling down or running into another player or the wall while trying to make the catch. [2.00]

Other reasons a batter may be called out are:

· failing to get into the proper position promptly after being called by the umpire; [6.06]
· stepping into the batter's box with or using an illegal bat—*Out!* [6.06]

· stepping from one batter's box to the other when the pitcher is ready; [6.06]

· after hitting a fair ball and moving toward first base, being hit by the ball before a fielder has a chance to make a play on it; [6.06]

27

- **using the bat to hit a fair ball a second time; (However, if the bat has been dropped and the umpire thinks the batter didn't intend to hit the ball the second time, the batter is not out and play continues.) [6.05]**

- **interfering with a catcher trying to make the play; [6.06]**

• a base runner touching a batted ball on purpose or interfering with a fielder trying to field the ball; [6.05]

• a teammate batting out of order, taking and completing the batter's turn at bat. If this happens the batting order resumes with the next batter listed after the improper one. If the mistake is discovered during an improper batter's turn at bat, the proper batter is inserted and the number of balls and/or strikes that have been called on the wrong batter will be applied to the proper batter. All the action (stolen bases, balks, etc.) that happened while an improper batter was at bat is considered fair. This is an appeal play—more on those later. (p.58) [6.07]

The Infield Fly Rule

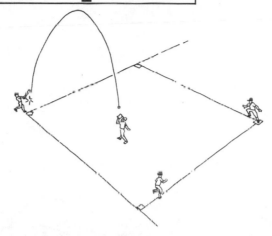

An infield fly is a fair fly ball that can be easily caught by an infielder. The batter is called out for hitting an infield fly when there are fewer than two outs and there are runners on first and second or first, second, and third. [2.00]

This seemingly bizarre rule is in place so that fielders will not drop an easily caught ball on purpose to set up a double play. In a double play, the defensive team gets the batter out and during the same play also puts out a runner that was forced to change bases by the batter's hit. A triple play would be getting out the batter and two runners.

If the umpire thinks a fielder has, for the same reason, intentionally dropped a line drive—that is, a hard hit ball that travels in a straight line—the batter is out.

WHEN THE BATTER BECOMES A BASE RUNNER

When the batter becomes a base runner and touches all the bases legally, a run is scored.

Three of the most common ways for a batter to become a base runner are:

• A fair ball is hit. [6.09] A fair ball is a batted ball that settles on fair ground. It may bounce on first or third base, on the foul line, or past third or first, and it will be fair.

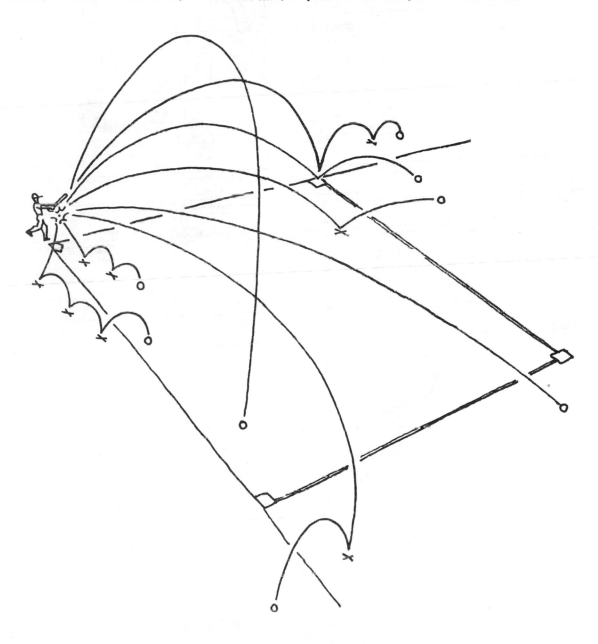

HOME RUN

HOME RUN

FAIR BALL

FAIR BALL

FOUL POLE

13

Whether a ball is fair or foul will be decided by the foul line and not by where the fielder is standing when the ball is touched. [2.00]
• A home run is hit over the outfield fence; the batter must still touch all the bases. [6.09]

- **Four balls are called by the ump. The batter becomes a runner, may walk to first base, and *cannot be put out*. [6.08]**

Awarded Bases

Besides four balls being called, there are other reasons a batter is awarded bases without having made a fair hit. One common way is if the batter is touched by a pitch. This does not mean that batters may throw themselves in front of a pitch to be awarded a base; the batter must try to avoid being hit by the pitch. If the batter *does not* try to avoid a ball that hits him outside the strike zone, then a "ball" is called. Furthermore, as stated earlier, a strike will be called if a pitch hits the batter in the strike zone. [6.08]

Other reasons a batter may be awarded bases are:

• If the catcher—or any fielder—interferes with the batter, the batter will be given first base and can't be put out. [6.08]

- If a fair ball accidentally touches a base runner before a fielder has a chance to make a play on it, the batter is given first base. (The runner, by the way, is out.) [6.08]

• **If a fairly hit ball hits an umpire before a fielder has had a chance to make a play on it, the batter is given one base. (If it hits the umpire after passing the fielder, the ball is live and play continues.) [6.08]**

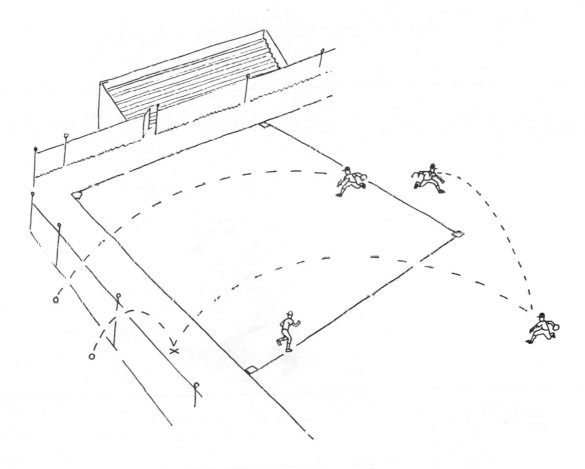

Sometimes more than one base is awarded the batter. For example:

- If a ball thrown by a fielder goes out of play—into the stands or lodges in the fence—
the batter is awarded two bases. If the throw was the first action of the play—other than
the pitcher's throw and the hit—the two bases will be the next two from where the
runners began, meaning that the player on first, for example, would go to third. If the
throw comes later in the play, the two bases are awarded from the last base each
runner legally reached—meaning that, although a player may have been on first at the
beginning of the play, if he'd advanced to second by the time the wild throw was made,
he'd be given third and home. [7.05]

- Three bases are awarded to the batter if a fielder tries to knock down a batted ball by throwing a glove or hat at it. The award will be four bases if the ball is interfered with in this way while it was going over the fence for a homer. [7.05]
- If there is interference from a spectator, such as leaning over or running onto the field, or any similar type of interference, the umpire may award bases or take any steps deemed necessary to nullify the interference. [3.16]

There are other times when batters and runners may be awarded bases, and they will be touched on in the base-running section. (p.54).

The Third Strike Rule

The third strike rule is one of the oldest in baseball, left over from the days when pitchers weren't supposed to pitch hard and catchers had no gloves. With all the changes that have occurred since then, it has become a sort of wild-card rule that injects an extra element of excitement into the game. Under this rule, three strikes do *not* always make an out. If (1) first base is unoccupied, or (2) first base is occupied with two outs, and in either case the catcher drops the third strike, the batter is not out, but may run. The catcher may try to pick up the ball and throw to first for the out. If there is a runner on first base or it is not the third out of the inning, then the rule does not go into effect. The reason for this is to ensure that the catcher won't drop the third-strike pitch on purpose to set up a double play. [6.09]

Base Runners

The runner must touch first, second, third, and home bases in order to score a run. [7.02, 5.06] A run is not scored if the runner has not touched home base by the time the third out is made to end an inning. Also, runs are not scored if any other runner is *forced* out for the third out. For example, if there are two outs and the batter hits a fair grounder but is quickly thrown out at first, and in the meantime the player on third has run home, that's no run—and the inning is over. [4.09]

A runner may not score if the third out is on an appeal play on a preceding runner. More on appeal plays later. (p.58) [7.10]

WHEN A RUNNER MAY RUN, WHEN A RUNNER MUST RUN

A base runner gains the right to a base by touching it before being put out. The base runner may then hold the base until either legally touching the next base or being forced to vacate by the runner following him. [7.01]

When a player at bat becomes a base runner, the runner already on first base *must* vacate that base and move along to second. If at this time there is also a runner holding second, that runner now must move along, and the same holds true for the player who's on third.

However, base runners are not forced to run if there's no runner advancing from the preceding base. If first base is empty, there's a player on second, and the batter makes a hit—the batter must run of course, but if staying on second seems prudent, the player on second may do so. [7.01]

When a batter is awarded a base or bases—rather than earning it through a hit—none of the runners who are compelled to move to the next base may be put out. [7.04]

43

These rules that force the base holders to move along exist in part because two runners may not occupy the same base at the same time. If it is not a forced situation, the first runner has the right to the base. For example, if the runner on first steals second, but the runner on second fails to move on to third, the latter is safe but the former may be tagged out. [7.03]

Anytime the ball is live, runners may step away from the base toward the next base. This is called "taking a lead" and might develop into an attempt to steal a base. However, if they're away from their base, they can be tagged out. Runners may run on fly balls that are caught, fair or foul. But if a fly is hit and caught, they must go back and tag the base before they can try to make a run for the next one. [7.08] When a foul ball is not caught, the ball is dead and no one runs until pitcher and catcher are ready to pitch. [5.09]

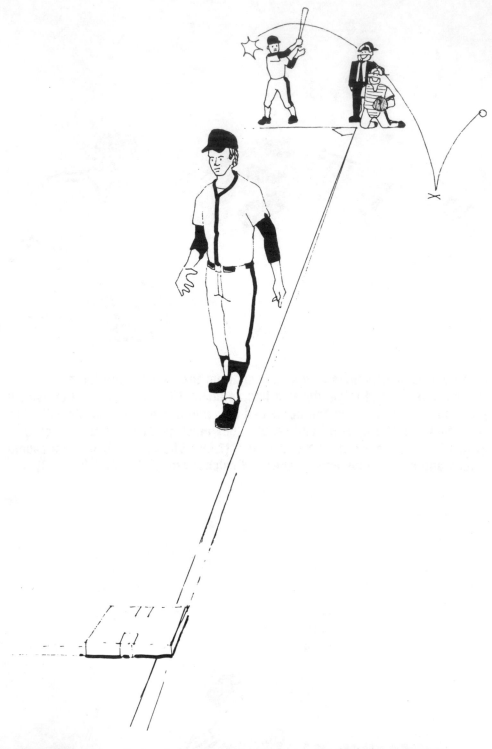

Generally, when the ball is live and play is in progress, runners may advance or be put out, but there are a number of reasons the ball will be considered dead. Sometimes during dead-ball situations, the runners may be awarded bases; other times they must return to the previous base. The most common situations are: [5.01]

- If a foul ball is hit and not caught, the runners must return to base. [5.09] Otherwise the batter would stand at the plate and hit foul balls all day while the runners looked for chances to advance around the bases.
- If a batter is hit by a pitch in such a way that he's entitled to first, the runners advance only if forced. [5.09]
- If a fielder falls (not steps) into a dugout with the ball runners are awarded one base. [5.10]

- If a ball is thrown off the field or into the stands, runners are awarded bases.
- If a player is injured. [5.10]
- If the manager asks for and gets a time out for a substitution. [5.10]
- If the umpire calls time; the umpire will almost never do this while play is in progress. [5.10]
- If the umpire accidentally interferes with the catcher's throw, then the ball is dead and the runners may not advance.

WHEN A BASE RUNNER IS OUT

The two most common ways for a base runner to be put out are:

- A fielder, while holding the ball securely in hand or glove, steps on or touches the base toward which a runner is forced, or touches the runner with the hand holding the ball. The runner's out! Runners may advance only if awarded bases by the umpire. [7.08]

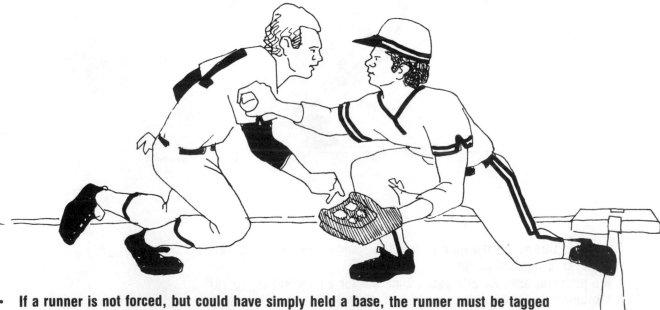

- If a runner is not forced, but could have simply held a base, the runner must be tagged out on the body while off base. The runner may not be put out by tagging a base. This is true even if a runner was, seconds before, being forced, but, due to the fact that the runner behind is now out, is no longer being forced. [7.08]

It's important to note that while a runner who overruns first base may *not* be tagged out, the runner overrunning or oversliding second or third *may* be put out. The runner, in sprinting past first, should be careful to turn right, not left, and return immediately to that base, otherwise the runner may be considered to be trying for second and may be tagged out, as shown in the illustration. The runner has beaten the throw to first but has turned In such a way that he now appears to be going for second base. He now may be tagged out. [7.10]

Other than the usual ways, there are some other less-common situations where a base runner will be called out:

- A runner may be called out if a fair ball touches the runner before a fielder has a chance to make a play on it. [7.08]
- A runner is out if, after a foul hit or bunt, the runner tries to touch the ball and change its path. The ball is dead, and no runners may advance. [7.09]

- Runners who intentionally interfere with a thrown ball or with a fielder will also be called out. [7.08] Runners may never interfere with a fielder's right to play the ball. The rules specify this because it is easier for the runner to watch and move around the fielder than for the fielder to watch and move out of the way of the runner while watching and fielding the ball. Runners who are already out may not loiter around the base and interfere with the play. If a runner interferes with a later play, the following runner will also be called out. [7.09]

- **The runner will be out if, to get away from a tag, he runs more than three feet away from the line between the bases. [7.08]**

- **Runners may not leave the base lines or they're out. The exception to this rule occurs when a runner has advanced but must return because the ball is dead; then staying within the baseline is not mandatory. If a runner must return to a base while the ball is live (for example if a runner missed a base and then realized his error) that runner must return along the base path. [7.02]**

If a base runner passes a foreward runner who is not out, the passing runner not only is not paying attention, but is OUT. [7.08]

• Runners may also be called out on appeal plays. For example, a runner or base may be tagged and then it may be pointed out to the umpire that the runner missed the base. It will not be automatically called by the umpire if a runner misses a base. The fielders must keep a sharp watch and speak up. This goes for home plate also. [7.10] More on appeal plays later. (p.58)

Other Awarded Bases

Some situations where base runners may advance one base without risk of being put out are:

- if a pitch is thrown into the stands; [7.05]

- if the batter is walked to first, forcing the other runner(s) to the next base(s); [7.04]
- if a wild pitch (a pitch that gets away from the pitcher and flies out of play) is thrown;

- if a fielder catches the ball and then, still holding the ball, falls into the stands or dugout; [7.04]
- or if a balk is committed. [7.04]

In some cases, runners may be awarded two bases:

- if a fair ball bounces or is deflected into the stands or if it becomes stuck in bushes or the fence; (The batter gets two bases also.) [7.05]
- when a thrown ball goes into the stands. If the runner has already gained bases when the throw was made into the stands, the runner gets two more bases from where he is.
- if a fielder hits a thrown ball while it is in play with a thrown glove or hat; [7.05]
- or if a fielder catches a thrown ball with a hat while the ball is in play. [7.05]

There are even some ways in which base runners may advance three bases without danger of being put out:

- when a member of the opposing team throws a glove at a fair batted ball or if a fielder catches the ball with a hat, mask, or any other part of the uniform; [7.05]
- or if a fielder throws his glove to deflect a ball going over the fence, the batter is awarded a home run. [7.05]

Obstruction

If the defensive players—the fielders, pitcher, and catcher of the team that is not playing the ball—won't let runners run the base paths, that's obstruction.

In cases of obstruction, intentional or not, the umpire awards all runners the bases that he thinks they would have reached, had there been no obstruction. The obstructed runner must be awarded at least one base beyond the last one that was legally touched. If the obstruction takes place in the midst of a play being made on the runner, the ball is dead then and there and that runner is awarded at least one base. If no play is being made on the obstructed runner, the play will be allowed to continue; only after all the action is completed will the umpire impose penalties. [7.06]

If the catcher interferes with the batter when a runner is stealing home, the batter is awarded first and the runner is awarded home.

If a spectator interferes with a live ball, the umpire will impose penalties or award as many bases as he thinks the runners would have achieved without the interference. The ball is dead. [3.16.]

No interference is allowed if a player reaches over a rail or fence into the crowd to try to make a catch. [2.00]

APPEAL PLAYS

An appeal takes place when a fielder claims to the umpire that the offensive team has violated the rules and that an out should be called against the violator. It must be made to the umpire before the next pitch to the batter, or before the next play (such as an attempt to catch a runner off base). Some plays that the defensive team must appeal in order to get an out are: [7.10]

- hitting with an illegal bat;
- failing to touch base after a fly ball is caught; if runner or base is tagged, the runner is out; [7.10]

- missing a base if the base is subsequently tagged;
- failing to return to first after overrunning it; [7.10]

- missing home; the runner must be tagged out unless he or she has already returned to the dugout, and then home may be tagged; [7.10]
- batting out of turn; the legal batter is out but the improper batter is not. [6.07]

UMPIRES

The home plate umpire is in charge of the game and all other umpires. The second in command is the field umpire, who may position himself anywhere on the field. [9.04] Before the game this umpire must see that the field is in proper condition and collect batting orders and lineups from the managers. The umpire is in complete charge and authority once the game has started and may even make decisions on situations not specifically covered in the rules. [9.01]

An umpire may be questioned about points of the rules, but his judgment about what happened in a given play may never be questioned. [9.02] An umpire may ask the other umpires in the field for help in making the call. No player or manager may disparage or, of course, touch the umpire or they will be ejected from the game. The umpire has the authority to order anyone associated with the game to refrain from doing anything which interferes with the application of the rules; he may disqualify any manager, coach, or player. [9.01]

It is also the umpire's duty to suspend the game when it is no longer safe or possible to play. This is most commonly done for rain, but might also be done in case of lightning, spectator rioting, earthquakes, etc. [4.12]

SAFE

STRIKE

TIME OUT

OUT

Here are some of the umpire's signals:

- "Out": Right fist is clenched, arm is raised. This signal should be made without hesitation.

- "Safe": Both arms are extended in front of the body, palms down. The position should be held long enough to be seen by players, managers, and other umpires.

- "Time": Arms are extended above the head, palms out. This position is held until the ump is satisfied that the signal has been seen and observed.

- "Strike": The right arm and hand are moved outward from the body and at least waist high.

Balls are not signaled, just called vocally.

Statistician

People often say that baseball is a game of statistics, and it is true that the official scorer keeps many records—much more than simply the number of runs.

One important statistic is "errors." It's the record of the number of mistakes made by each fielder during the game. An error is charged for each mistake, missed catch, or wild throw that keeps a runner from being put out, or lets a runner take more bases. Among the fans in the stands, it is sometimes a matter of great controversy whether or not an action was or should have been considered an error, and by whom an error was committed. But once the statistician has recorded it as an error, it's an error. These records, while of interest for many reasons, have no effect on the way the game will be played or who will win.

AFTERWORD

Dino, by the way, whom we mentioned in the foreword, could not have picked a better year than the one he did (1986) to meet baseball: The Mets won the series that year, and he was hooked. Dino's friend, sadly, moved away soon thereafter. But a couple of Junes later that friend called Dino while on a visit to the Big Apple and asked for a lift from the airport. There was a pause on the line and then finally Dino said, "But, my friend, the *game* is on."

RULES

Reprinted with permission from Major League Properties, 1989.

2.00—Definitions of Terms.

(All definitions in Rule 2.00 are listed alphabetically.)

ADJUDGED is a judgment decision by the umpire.

An APPEAL is the act of a fielder in claiming violation of the rules by the offensive team.

A BALK is an illegal act by the pitcher with a runner or runners on base, entitling all runners to advance one base.

A BALL is a pitch which does not enter the strike zone in flight and is not struck at by the batter.

If the pitch touches the ground and bounces through the strike zone it is a "ball." If such a pitch touches the batter, he shall be awarded first base. If the batter swings at such a pitch after two strikes, the ball cannot be caught, for the purposes of Rule 6.05 (c) and 6.09 (b). If the batter hits such a pitch, the ensuing action shall be the same as if he hit the ball in flight.

A BASE is one of four points which must be touched by a runner in order to score a run; more usually applied to the canvas bags and the rubber plate which mark the base points.

A BASE COACH is a team member in uniform who is stationed in the coach's box at first or third base to direct the batter and the runners.

A BASE ON BALLS is an award of first base granted to a batter who, during his time at bat, receives four pitches outside the strike zone.

A BATTER is an offensive player who takes his position in the batter's box.

BATTER-RUNNER is a term that identifies the offensive player who has just finished his time at bat until he is put out or until the play on which he became a runner ends.

The BATTER'S BOX is the area within which the batter shall stand during his time at bat.

The BATTERY is the pitcher and catcher.

BENCH or DUGOUT is the seating facilities reserved for players, substitutes and other team members in uniform when they are not actively engaged on the playing field.

A BUNT is a batted ball not swung at, but intentionally met with the bat and tapped slowly within the infield.

A CALLED GAME is one in which, for any reason, the umpire-in-chief terminates play.

A CATCH is the act of a fielder in getting secure possession in his hand or glove of a ball in flight and firmly holding it; providing he does not use his cap, protector, pocket or any other part of his uniform in getting possession. It is not a catch, however, if simultaneously or immediately following his contact with the ball, he collides with a player, or with a wall, or if he falls down, and as a result of such collision or falling, drops the ball. It is not a catch if a fielder touches a fly ball which then hits a member of the offensive team or an umpire and then is caught by another defensive player. If the fielder has made the catch and drops the ball while in the act of making a throw following the catch, the ball shall be adjudged to have been caught. In establishing the validity of the catch, the fielder shall hold the ball long enough to prove that he has complete control of the ball and that his release of the ball is voluntary and intentional.

A catch is legal if the ball is finally held by any fielder, even though juggled, or held by another fielder before it touches the ground. Runners may leave their bases the instant the first fielder touches the ball. A fielder may reach over a fence, railing, rope or other line of demarcation to make a catch. He may jump on top of a railing, or canvas that may be in foul ground. No interference should be allowed when a fielder reaches over a fence, railing, rope or into a stand to catch a ball. He does so at his own risk.

If a fielder, attempting a catch at the edge of the dugout, is "held up" and kept from an apparent fall by a player or players of either team and the catch is made, it shall be allowed.

The CATCHER is the fielder who takes his position back of the home base.

The CATCHER'S BOX is that area within which the catcher shall stand until the pitcher delivers the ball.

The CLUB is a person or group of persons responsible for assembling the team personnel, providing the playing field and required facilities, and representing the team in relations with the league.

A COACH is a team member in uniform appointed by the manager to perform such duties as the manager may designate, such as but not limited to acting as base coach.

A DEAD BALL is a ball out of play because of a legally created temporary suspension of play.

The DEFENSE (or DEFENSIVE) is the team, or any player of the team, in the field.

A DOUBLE-HEADER is two regularly scheduled or rescheduled games, played in immediate succession.

A DOUBLE PLAY is a play by the defense in which two offensive players are put out as a result of continuous action, providing there is no error between putouts.

(a) A force double play is one in which both putouts are force plays.

(b) A reverse force double play is one in which the first out is a force play and the second out is made on a runner for whom the force is removed by reason of the first out. Examples of reverse force plays: runner on first, one out; batter grounds to first baseman, who steps on first base (one out) and throws to second baseman or shortstop for the second out (a tag play).

Another example: bases loaded, none out; batter grounds to third baseman, who steps on third base (one out), then throws to catcher for the second out (tag play).

DUGOUT (see definition of BENCH).

A FAIR BALL is a batted ball that settles on fair ground between home and first base, or between home and third base, or that is on or over fair territory when bounding to the outfield past first or third base, or that touches first, second or third base, or that first falls on fair territory on or beyond first base or third base, or that, while on or over fair territory, touches the person of an umpire or player, or that, while over fair territory, passes out of the playing field in flight.

A fair fly shall be judged according to the relative position of the ball and the foul line, including the foul pole, and not as to whether the fielder is on fair or foul territory at the time he touches the ball.

If a fly ball lands in the infield between home and first base, or home and third base, and then bounces to foul territory without touching a player or umpire and before passing first or third base, it is a foul ball; or if the ball settles on foul territory or is touched by a player on foul territory, it is a foul ball. If a fly ball lands on or beyond first or third base and then bounces to foul territory, it is a fair hit.

Clubs, increasingly, are erecting tall foul poles at the fence line with a wire netting extending along the side of the pole on fair territory above the fence to enable the umpires more accurately to judge fair and foul balls.

FAIR TERRITORY is that part of the playing field within, and including the first base and third base lines, from home base to the bottom of the playing field fence and perpendicularly upwards. All foul lines are in fair territory.

A FIELDER is any defensive player.

FIELDER'S CHOICE is the act of a fielder who handles a fair grounder and, instead of throwing to first base to put out the batter-runner, throws to another base in an attempt to put out a preceding runner. The term is also used by scorers (a) to account for the advance of the batter-runner who takes one or more extra bases when the fielder who handles his safe hit attempts to put out a preceding runner; (b) to account for the advance of a runner (other than by stolen base or error) while a fielder is attempting to put out another runner; and (c) to account for the advance of a runner made solely because of the defensive team's indifference (undefended steal).

A FLY BALL is a batted ball that goes high in the air in flight.

A FORCE PLAY is a play in which a runner legally loses his right to occupy a base by reason of the batter becoming a runner.

Confusion regarding this play is removed by remembering that frequently the "force" situation is removed during the play. Example: Man on first, one out, ball hit sharply to first baseman who touches the bag and batter-runner is out. The force is removed at that moment and runner advancing to second must be tagged. If there had been a runner on third or second, and either of these runners scored before the tag-out at second, the run counts. Had the first baseman thrown to second and the ball then had been returned to first, the play at second was a force out, making two outs, and the return throw to first ahead of the runner would have made three outs. In that case, no run would score.

Example: Not a force out. One out. Runner on first and third. Batter flies out. Two out. Runner on third tags up and scores. Runner on first tries to retouch before throw from fielder reaches first baseman, but does not get back in time and is out. Three outs. If, in umpire's judgment, the runner from third touched home before the ball was held at first base, the run counts.

A FORFEITED GAME is a game declared ended by the umpire-in-chief in favor of the offended team by the score of 9 to 0, for violation of the rules.

A FOUL BALL is a batted ball that settles on foul territory between home and first base, or between home and third base, or that bounds past first or third base on or over foul territory, or that first falls on foul territory beyond first or third base, or that, while on or over foul territory, touches the person of an umpire or player, or any object foreign to the natural ground.

A foul fly shall be judged according to the relative position of the ball and the foul line, including the foul pole, and not as to whether the fielder is on foul or fair territory at the time he touches the ball.

A batted ball not touched by a fielder, which hits the pitcher's rubber and rebounds into foul territory, between home and first, or between home and third base is a foul ball.

FOUL TERRITORY is that part of the playing field outside the first and third base lines extended to the fence and perpendicularly upwards.

A FOUL TIP is a batted ball that goes sharp and direct from the bat to the catcher's hands and is legally caught. It is not a foul tip unless caught and any foul tip that is caught is a strike, and the ball is in play. It is not a catch if it is a rebound, unless the ball has first touched the catcher's glove or hand.

A GROUND BALL is a batted ball that rolls or bounces close to the ground.

The HOME TEAM is the team on whose grounds the game is played, or if the game is played on neutral grounds, the home team shall be designated by mutual agreement.

ILLEGAL (or ILLEGALLY) is contrary to these rules.

An ILLEGAL PITCH is (1) a pitch delivered to the batter when the pitcher does not have his pivot foot in contact with the pitcher's plate; (2) a quick return pitch. An illegal pitch when runners are on base is a balk.

An INFIELDER is a fielder who occupies a position in the infield.

An INFIELD FLY is a fair fly ball (not including a line drive or an attempted bunt) which can be caught by an infielder with ordinary effort, when first and second, or first, second and third bases are occupied, before two are out. The pitcher, catcher and any outfielder who stations himself in the infield on the play shall be considered infielders for the purpose of this rule.

When it seems apparent that a batted ball will be an Infield Fly, the umpire shall immediately declare "Infield Fly" for the benefit of the runners. If the ball is near the baselines, the umpire shall declare "Infield Fly, if Fair."

The ball is alive and runners may advance at the risk of the ball being caught, or retouch and advance after the ball is touched, the same as on any fly ball. If the hit becomes a foul ball, it is treated the same as any foul.

If a declared Infield Fly is allowed to fall untouched to the ground, and bounces foul before passing first or third base, it is a foul ball. If a declared Infield Fly falls untouched to the ground outside the baseline, and bounces fair before passing first or third base, it is an Infield Fly.

On the Infield Fly rule the umpire is to rule whether the ball could ordinarily have been handled by an infielder—not by some arbitrary limitation such as the grass, or the base lines. The umpire must rule also that a ball is an Infield Fly, even if handled by an outfielder, if, in the umpire's judgment, the ball could have been as easily handled by an infielder. The Infield Fly is in no sense to be considered an appeal play. The umpire's judgment must govern, and the decision should be made immediately.

When an Infield Fly rule is called, runners may advance at their own risk. If on an Infield Fly rule, the infielder intentionally drops a fair ball, the ball remains in play despite the provisions of Rule 6.05 (L). The Infield Fly rule takes precedence.

IN FLIGHT describes a batted, thrown, or pitched ball which has not yet touched the ground or some object other than a fielder.

IN JEOPARDY is a term indicating that the ball is in play and an offensive player may be put out.

An INNING is that portion of a game within which the teams alternate on offense and defense and in which there are three putouts for each team. Each team's time at bat is a half-inning.

INTERFERENCE

(a) Offensive interference is an act by the team at bat which interferes with, obstructs, impedes, hinders or confuses any fielder attempting to make a play. If the umpire declares the batter, batter-runner, or a runner out for interference, all other runners shall return to the last base that was, in the judgment of the umpire, legally touched at the time of the interference, unless otherwise provided by these rules.

In the event the batter-runner has not reached first base, all runners shall return to the base last occupied at the time of the pitch.

(b) Defensive interference is an act by a fielder which hinders or prevents a batter from hitting a pitch.

(c) Umpire's interference occurs (1) when an umpire hinders, impedes or prevents a catcher's throw attempting to prevent a stolen base, or (2) when a fair ball touches an umpire on fair territory before passing a fielder.

(d) Spectator interference occurs when a spectator reaches out of the stands, or goes on the playing field, and touches a live ball.

On any interference the ball is dead.

The LEAGUE is a group of Clubs whose teams play each other in a pre-arranged schedule under these rules for the league championship.

The LEAGUE PRESIDENT shall enforce the official rules, resolve any disputes involving the rules, and determine any protested games. The league president may fine or suspend any player, coach, manager or umpire for violation of these rules, at his discretion.

LEGAL (or LEGALLY) is in accordance with these rules.

A LIVE BALL is a ball which is in play.

A LINE DRIVE is a batted ball that goes sharp and direct from the bat to a fielder without touching the ground.

The MANAGER is a person appointed by the Club to be responsible for the team's actions on the field, and to represent the team in communications with the umpire and the opposing team. A player may be appointed manager.

(a) The Club shall designate the manager to the league president or the umpire-in-chief not less than thirty minutes before the scheduled starting time of the game.

(b) The manager may advise the umpire that he has delegated specific duties prescribed by the rules to a player or coach, and any action of such designated representative shall be official. The manager shall always be responsible for his team's conduct, observance of the official rules, and deference to the umpires.

(c) If a manager leaves the field, he shall designate a player or coach as his substitute; and such substitute manager shall have the duties, rights and responsibilities of the manager. If the manager fails or refuses to designate his substitute before leaving, the umpire-in-chief shall designate a team member as substitute manager.

OBSTRUCTION is the act of a fielder who, while not in possession of the ball and not in the act of fielding the ball, impedes the progress of any runner.

If a fielder is about to receive a thrown ball and if the ball is in flight directly toward and near enough to the fielder so he must occupy his position to receive the ball he may be considered "in the act of fielding a ball." It is entirely up to the judgment of the umpire as to whether a fielder is in the act of fielding a ball. After a fielder has made an attempt to field a ball and missed, he can no longer be in the "act of fielding" the ball. For example: an infielder dives at a ground ball and the ball passes him and he continues to lie on the ground and delays the progress of the runner, he very likely has obstructed the runner.

OFFENSE is the team, or any player of the team, at bat.

OFFICIAL SCORER. See Rule 10.00.

An OUT is one of the three required retirements of an offensive team during its time at bat.

An OUTFIELDER is a fielder who occupies a position in the outfield, which is the area of the playing field most distant from home base.

OVERSLIDE (or OVERSLIDING) is the act of an offensive player when his slide to a base, other than when advancing from home to first base, is with such momentum that he loses contact with the base.

A PENALTY is the application of these rules following an illegal act.

The PERSON of a player or an umpire is any part of his body, his clothing or his equipment.

A PITCH is a ball delivered to the batter by the pitcher.

All other deliveries of the ball by one player to another are thrown balls.

A PITCHER is the fielder designated to deliver the pitch to the batter.

The pitcher's PIVOT FOOT is that foot which is in contact with the pitcher's plate as he delivers the pitch.

"PLAY" is the umpire's order to start the game or to resume action following any dead ball.

A QUICK RETURN pitch is one made with obvious intent to catch a batter off balance. It is an illegal pitch.

REGULATION GAME. See Rules 4.10 and 4.11.

A RETOUCH is the act of a runner in returning to a base as legally required.

A RUN (or SCORE) is the score made by an offensive player who advances from batter to runner and touches first, second, third and home bases in that order.

A RUN-DOWN is the act of the defense in an attempt to put out a runner between bases.

A RUNNER is an offensive player who is advancing toward, or touching, or returning to any base.

"SAFE" is a declaration by the umpire that a runner is entitled to the base for which he was trying.

SET POSITION is one of the two legal pitching positions.

SQUEEZE PLAY is a term to designate a play when a team, with a runner on third base, attempts to score that runner by means of a bunt.

A STRIKE is a legal pitch when so called by the umpire, which—

(a) Is struck at by the batter and is missed;

(b) Is not struck at, if any part of the ball passes through any part of the strike zone;

(c) Is fouled by the batter when he has less than two strikes;

(d) Is bunted foul;

(e) Touches the batter as he strikes at it;

(f) Touches the batter in flight in the strike zone; or

(g) Becomes a foul tip.

The STRIKE ZONE is that area over home plate the upper limit of which is a horizontal line at the midpoint between the top of the shoulders and the top of the uniform pants, and the lower level is a line at the top of the knees. The Strike Zone shall be determined from the batter's stance as the batter is prepared to swing at a pitched ball.

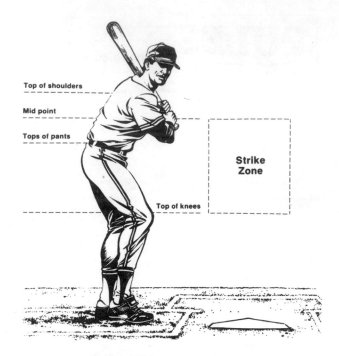

Top of shoulders

Mid point

Tops of pants

Strike Zone

Top of knees

A SUSPENDED GAME is a called game which is to be completed at a later date.

A TAG is the action of a fielder in touching a base with his body while holding the ball securely and firmly in his hand or glove; or touching a runner with the ball, or with his hand or glove holding the ball, while holding the ball securely and firmly in his hand or glove.

A THROW is the act of propelling the ball with the hand and arm to a given objective and is to be distinguished, always, from the pitch.

A TIE GAME is a regulation game which is called when each team has the same number of runs.

"TIME" is the announcement by an umpire of a legal interruption of play, during which the ball is dead.

TOUCH. To touch a player or umpire is to touch any part of his body, his clothing or his equipment.

A TRIPLE PLAY is a play by the defense in which three offensive players are put out as a result of continuous action, providing there is no error between putouts.

A WILD PITCH is one so high, so low, or so wide of the plate that it cannot be handled with ordinary effort by the catcher.

WIND-UP POSITION is one of the two legal pitching positions.

3.00—Game Preliminaries.

3.01 Before the game begins the umpire shall—

(a) Require strict observance of all rules governing implements of play and equipment of players;

(b) Be sure that all playing lines (heavy lines on Diagrams No. 1 and No. 2) are marked with lime, chalk or other white material easily distinguishable from the ground or grass;

(c) Receive from the home Club a supply of regulation baseballs, the number and make to be certified to the home Club by the league president. Each ball shall be enclosed in a sealed package bearing the signature of the league president, and the seal shall not be broken until just prior to game time when the umpire shall open each package to inspect the ball and remove its gloss. The umpire shall be the sole judge of the fitness of the balls to be used in the game;

(d) Be assured by the home Club that at least one dozen regulation reserve balls are immediately available for use if required;

(e) Have in his possession at least two alternate balls and shall require replenishment of such supply of alternate balls as needed throughout the game. Such alternate balls shall be put in play when—

(1) A ball has been batted out of the playing field or into the spectator area;

(2) A ball has become discolored or unfit for further use;

(3) The pitcher requests such alternate ball.

The umpire shall not give an alternate ball to the pitcher until play has ended and the previously used ball is dead. After a thrown or batted ball goes out of the playing field, play shall not be resumed with an alternate ball until the runners have reached the bases to which they are entitled. After a home run is hit out of the playing grounds, the umpire shall not deliver a new ball to the pitcher or the catcher until the batter hitting the home run has crossed the plate.

3.02 No player shall intentionally discolor or damage the ball by rubbing it with soil, rosin, paraffin, licorice, sand-paper, emery-paper or other foreign substance.

PENALTY: The umpire shall demand the ball and remove the offender from the game. In case the umpire cannot locate the offender, and if the pitcher delivers such discolored or damaged ball to the batter, the pitcher shall be removed from the game at once and shall be suspended automatically for ten days.

3.03 A player, or players, may be substituted during a game at any time the ball is dead. A substitute player shall bat in the replaced player's position in the team's batting order. A player once removed from a game shall not re-enter that game. If a substitute enters the game in place of a player-manager, the manager may thereafter go to the coaching lines at his discretion. When two or more substitute players of the defensive team enter the game at the same time, the manager shall, immediately before they take their positions as fielders, designate to the umpire-in-chief such players' positions in the team's batting order and the umpire-in-chief shall so notify the official scorer. If this information is not immediately given to the umpire-in-chief, he shall have authority to designate the substitutes' places in the batting order.

A pitcher may change to another position only once during the same inning; e.g. the pitcher will not be allowed to assume a position other than a pitcher more than once in the same inning.

Any player other than a pitcher substituted for an injured player shall be allowed five warm-up throws. (See Rule 8.03 for pitchers.)

3.04 A player whose name is on his team's batting order may not become a substitute runner for another member of his team.

This rule is intended to eliminate the practice of using so-called courtesy runners. No player in the game shall be permitted to act as a courtesy runner for a teammate. No player who has been in the game and has been taken out for a substitute shall return as a courtesy runner. Any player not in the lineup, if used as a runner, shall be considered as a substitute player.

3.05 (a) The pitcher named in the batting order handed the umpire-in-chief, as provided in Rules 4.01 (a) and 4.01 (b), shall pitch to the first batter or any substitute batter until such batter is put out or reaches first base, unless the pitcher sustains injury or illness which, in the judgment of the umpire-in-chief, incapacitates him from pitching.

(b) If the pitcher is replaced, the substitute pitcher shall pitch to the batter then at bat, or any substitute batter, until such batter is put out or reaches first base, or until the offensive team is put out, unless the substitute pitcher sustains injury or illness which, in the umpire-in-chief's judgment, incapacitates him for further play as a pitcher.

(c) If an improper substitution is made for the pitcher, the umpire shall direct the proper pitcher to return to the game until the provisions of this rule are fulfilled. If the improper pitcher is permitted to pitch, any play that results is legal. The improper pitcher becomes the proper pitcher as soon as he makes his first pitch to the batter, or as soon as any runner is put out.

If a manager attempts to remove a pitcher in violation of Rule 3.05 (c) the umpire shall notify the manager of the offending Club that it cannot be done. If, by chance, the umpire-in-chief has, through oversight, announced the incoming improper pitcher, he should still correct the situation before the improper pitcher pitches. Once the improper pitcher delivers a pitch he becomes the proper pitcher.

3.06 The manager shall immediately notify the umpire-in-chief of any substitution and shall state to the umpire-in-chief the substitute's place in his batting order.

Players for whom substitutions have been made may remain with their team on the bench or may "warm-up" pitchers. If a manager substitutes another player for himself, he may continue to direct his team from the bench or the coach's box. Umpires should not permit players for whom substitutes have been made, and who are permitted to remain on the bench, to address any remarks to any opposing player or manager, or to the umpires.

3.07 The umpire-in-chief, after having been notified, shall immediately announce, or cause to be announced, each substitution.

3.08 (a) If no announcement of a substitution is made, the substitute shall be considered as having entered the game when—

(1) If a pitcher, he takes his place on the pitcher's plate;

(2) If a batter, he takes his place in the batter's box;

(3) If a fielder, he reaches the position usually occupied by the fielder he has replaced, and play commences;

(4) If a runner, he takes the place of the runner he has replaced.

(b) Any play made by, or on, any of the above mentioned unannounced substitutes shall be legal.

3.09 Players in uniform shall not address or mingle with spectators, nor sit in the stands before, during, or after a game. No manager, coach or player shall address any spectator before or during a game. Players of opposing teams shall not fraternize at any time while in uniform.

3.10 (a) The manager of the home team shall be the sole judge as to whether a game shall be started because of unsuitable weather conditions or the unfit condition of the playing field, except for the second game of a doubleheader. EXCEPTION: Any league may permanently authorize its president to suspend the application of this rule as to that league during the closing weeks of its championship season in order to assure that the championship is decided each year on its merits. When the postponement of, and possible failure to play, a game in the final series of a championship season between any two teams might affect the final standing of any Club in the league, the president, on appeal from any league Club, may assume the authority granted the home team manager by this rule.

(b) The umpire-in-chief of the first game shall be the sole judge as to whether the second game of a doubleheader shall not be started because of unsuitable weather conditions or the unfit condition of the playing field.

(c) The umpire-in-chief shall be the sole judge as to whether and when play shall be suspended during a game because of unsuitable weather conditions or the unfit condition of the playing field; as to whether and when they play shall be resumed after such suspenion; and as to whether and when a game shall be terminated after such suspenion. He shall not call the game until at least thirty minutes after he has suspended play. He may continue the suspension as long as he believes there is any chance to resume play.

The umpire-in-chief shall at all times try to complete a game. His authority to resume play following one or more suspensions of as much as thirty minutes each shall be absolute and he shall terminate a game only when there appears to be no possibility of completing it.

3.11 Between games of a doubleheader, or whenever a game is suspended because of the unfitness of the playing field, the umpire-in-chief shall have control of groundskeepers and assistants for the purpose of making the playing field fit for play.

PENALTY: For violation, the umpire in chief may forfeit the game to the visiting team.

3.12 When the umpire suspends play he shall call "Time." At the umpire's call of "Play," the suspension is lifted and play resumes. Between the call of "Time" and the call of "Play" the ball is dead.

3.13 The manager of the home team shall present to the umpire-in-chief and the opposing manager any ground rules he thinks necessary covering the overflow of spectators upon the playing field, batted or thrown balls into such overflow, or any other contingencies. If these rules are acceptable to the opposing manager they shall be legal. If these rules are unacceptable to the opposing manager, the umpire-in-chief shall make and enforce any special ground rules he thinks are made necessary by ground conditions, which shall not conflict with the official playing rules.

3.14 Members of the offensive team shall carry all gloves and other equipment off the field and to the dugout while their team is at bat. No equipment shall be left lying on the field, either in fair or foul territory.

3.15 No person shall be allowed on the playing field during a game except players and coaches in uniform, managers, news photographers authorized by the home team, umpires, officers of the law in uniform and watchmen or other employees of the home club. In case of unintentional interference with play by any person herein authorized to be on the playing field (except members of the offensive team participating in the game, or a coach in the coach's box, or an umpire) the ball is alive and in play. If the interference is intentional, the ball shall be dead at the moment of the interference and the umpire shall impose such penalties as in his opinion will nullify the act of interference.

NOTE: See Rule 7.11 for individuals excepted above; also see Rule 7.08 (b).

The question of intentional or unintentional interference shall be decided on the basis of the person's action. For example: a batboy, ball attendant, policeman, etc., who tries to avoid being touched by a thrown or batted ball but still is touched by the ball would be involved in unintentional interference. If, however, he kicks the ball or picks it up or pushes it, that is considered intentional interference, regardless of what his thought may have been.

PLAY: Batter hits ball to shortstop, who fields ball but throws wild past first baseman. The offensive coach at first base, to avoid being hit by the ball, falls to the ground and the first baseman on his way to retrieve the wild thrown ball, runs into the coach; the batter-runner finally ends up on third base. The question is asked whether the umpire should call interference on the part of the coach. This would be up to the judgment of the umpire and if the umpire felt that the coach did all he could to avoid interfering with the play, no interference need be called. If it appeared to the umpire that the coach was obviously just making it appear he was trying not to interfere, the umpire should rule interference.

3.16 When there is spectator interference with any thrown or batted ball, the ball shall be dead at the moment of interference and the umpire shall impose such penalties as in his opinion will nullify the act of interference.

APPROVED RULING: If spectator interference clearly prevents a fielder from catching a fly ball, the umpire shall declare the batter out.

There is a difference between a ball which has been thrown or batted into the stands, touching a spectator thereby being out of play, even though it rebounds onto the field and a spectator going onto the field or reaching over, under or through a barrier and touching a ball in play or touching or otherwise interfering with a player. In the latter case it is clearly intentional and shall be dealt with as intentional interference as in Rule 3.15. Batter and runners shall be placed where in the umpire's judgment they would have been had the interference not occurred.

No interference shall be allowed when a fielder reaches over a fence, railing, rope or into a stand to catch a ball. He does so at his own risk. However, should a spectator reach out on the playing field side of such fence, railing or rope, and plainly prevent the fielder from catching the ball, then the batsman should be called out for the spectator's interference.

Example: Runner on third base, one out and a batter hits a fly ball deep to the outfield (fair or foul). Spectator clearly interferes with the outfielder attempting to catch the fly ball. Umpire calls the batter out for spectator interference. Ball is dead at the time of the call. Umpire decides that because of the distance the ball was hit, the runner on third base would have scored after the catch if the fielder had caught the ball which was interfered with; therefore, the runner is permitted to score. This might not be the case if such fly ball was interfered with a short distance from home plate.

3.17 Players and substitutes of both teams shall confine themselves to their team's benches unless actually participating in the play or preparing to enter the game, or coaching at first or third base. No one except players, substitutes, managers, coaches, trainers and bat boys shall occupy a bench during a game.

PENALTY: For violation the umpire may, after warning, remove the offender from the field.

Players on the disabled list are permitted to participate in pre-game activity and sit on the bench during a game but may not take part in any activity during the game such as warming up a pitcher, bench-jockeying, etc. Disabled players are not allowed to enter the playing surface at any time or for any purpose during the game.

3.18 The home team shall provide police protection sufficient to preserve order. If a person, or persons, enters the playing field during a game and interferes in any way with the play, the visiting team may refuse to play until the field is cleared.

PENALTY: If the field is not cleared in a reasonable length of time, which shall in no case be less than fifteen minutes after the visiting team's refusal to play, the umpire may forfeit the game to the visiting team.

4.00—Starting and Ending a Game.

4.01 Unless the home club shall have given previous notice that the game has been postponed or will be delayed in starting, the umpire, or umpires, shall enter the playing field five minutes before the hour set for the game to begin and proceed directly to home base where they shall be met by the managers of the opposing teams.

In sequence—

(a) First, the home manager shall give his batting order to the umpire-in-chief, in duplicate.

(b) Next, the visiting manager shall give his batting order to the umpire-in-chief, in duplicate.

(c) The umpire-in-chief shall make certain that the original and copies of the respective batting orders are identical, and then tender a copy of each batting order to the opposing manager. The copy retained by the umpire shall be the official batting order. The tender of the batting order by the umpire shall establish the batting orders. Thereafter, no substitutions shall be made by either manager, except as provided in these rules.

(d) As soon as the home team's batting order is handed to the umpire-in-chief the umpires are in charge of the playing field and from that moment they shall have sole authority to determine when a game shall be called, suspended or resumed on account of weather or the condition of the playing field.

Obvious errors in the batting order, which are noticed by the umpire-in-chief before he calls "Play" for the start of the game, should be called to the attention of the manager or captain of the team in error, so the correction can be made before the game starts. For example, if a manager has inadvertently listed only eight men in the batting order, or has listed two players with the same last name but without an identifying initial and the errors are noticed by the umpire before he calls "play," he shall cause such error or errors to be corrected before he calls "play" to start the game. Teams should not be "trapped" later by some mistake that obviously was inadvertent and which can be corrected before the game starts.

4.02 The players of the home team shall take their defensive positions, the first batter of the visiting team shall take his position in the batter's box, the umpire shall call "Play" and the game shall start.

4.03 When the ball is put in play at the start of, or during a game, all fielders other than the catcher shall be on fair territory.

(a) The catcher shall station himself directly back of the plate. He may leave his position at any time to catch a pitch or make a play except that when the batter is being given an intentional base on balls, the catcher must stand with both feet within the lines of the catcher's box until the ball leaves the pitcher's hand.

PENALTY: Balk.

(b) The pitcher, while in the act of delivering the ball to the batter, shall take his legal position;

(c) Except the pitcher and the catcher, any fielder may station himself anywhere in fair territory;

(d) Except the batter, or a runner attempting to score, no offensive player shall cross the catcher's lines when the ball is in play.

4.04 The batting order shall be followed throughout the game unless a player is substituted for another. In that case the substitute shall take the place of the replaced player in the batting order.

4.05 (a) The offensive team shall station two base coaches on the field during its term at bat, one near first base and one near third base.

(b) Base coaches shall be limited to two in number and shall (1) be in team uniform, and (2) remain within the coach's box at all times.

PENALTY: The offending base coach shall be removed from the game, and shall leave the playing field.

It has been common practice for many years for some coaches to put one foot outside the coach's box or stand astride or otherwise be slightly outside the coaching box lines. The coach shall not be considered out of the box unless the opposing manager complains, and then, the umpire shall strictly enforce the rule and require all coaches (on both teams) to remain in the coach's box at all times.

It is also common practice for a coach who has a play at his base to leave the coach's box to signal the player to slide, advance or return to a base. This may be allowed if the coach does not interfere with the play in any manner.

4.06 (a) No manager, player, substitute, coach, trainer or batboy shall at any time, whether from the bench, the coach's box or on the playing field, or elsewhere

(1) Incite, or try to incite, by word or sign a demonstration by spectators;
(2) Use language which will in any manner refer to or reflect upon opposing players, an umpire, or any spectator;
(3) Call "Time," or employ any other word or phrase or commit any act while the ball is alive and in play for the obvious purpose of trying to make the pitcher commit a balk.
(4) Make intentional contact with the umpire in any manner.

(b) No fielder shall take a position in the batter's line of vision, and with deliberate unsportsmanlike intent, act in a manner to distract the batter.

PENALTY: The offender shall be removed from the game and shall leave the playing field, and, if a balk is made, it shall be nullified.

4.07 When a manager, player, coach or trainer is ejected from a game, he shall leave the field immediately and take no further part in that game. He shall remain in the clubhouse or change to street clothes and either leave the park or take a seat in the grandstand well removed from the vicinity of his team's bench or bullpen.

If a manager, coach or player is under suspension he may not be in the dugout or press box during the course of a game.

4.08 When the occupants of a player's bench show violent disapproval of an umpire's decision, the umpire shall first give warning that such disapproval shall cease. If such action continues—

PENALTY: The umpire shall order the offenders from the bench to the clubhouse. If he is unable to detect the offender, or offenders, he may clear the bench of all substitute players. The manager of the offending team shall have the privilege of recalling to the playing field only those players needed for substitution in the game.

4.09 HOW A TEAM SCORES.

(a) One run shall be scored each time a runner legally advances to and touches first, second, third and home base before three men are put out to end the inning. EXCEPTION: A run is not scored if the runner advances to home base during a play in which the third out is made (1) by the batter-runner before he touches first base; (2) by any runner being forced out; or (3) by a preceding runner who is declared out because he failed to touch one of the bases.

(b) When the winning run is scored in the last half-inning of a regulation game, or in the last half of an extra inning, as the result of a base on balls, hit batter or any other play with the bases full which forces the runner on third to advance, the umpire shall not declare the game ended until the runner forced to advance from third has touched home base and the batter-runner has touched first base.

An exception will be if fans rush onto the field and physically prevent the runner from touching home plate or the batter from touching first base. In such cases, the umpires shall award the runner the base because of the obstruction by the fans.

PENALTY: If the runner on third refuses to advance to and touch home base in a reasonable time, the umpire shall disallow the run, call out the offending player and order the game resumed. If, with two out, the batter-runner refuses to advance to and touch first base, the umpire shall disallow the run, call out the offending player, and order the game resumed. If, before two are out, the batter-runner refuses to advance to and touch first base, the run shall count, but the offending player shall be called out.

Approved Ruling: No run shall score during a play in which the third out is made by the batter-runner before he touches first base. Example: One out, Jones on second, Smith on first. The batter, Brown, hits safely. Jones scores. Smith is out on the throw to plate. Two outs. But Brown missed first base. The ball is thrown to first, an appeal is made, and Brown is out. Three outs. Since Jones crossed the plate during a play in which the third out was made by the batter-runner before he touched first base, Jones' run does not count.

Approved Ruling: Following runners are not affected by an act of a preceding runner unless two are out.

Example: One out, Jones on second, Smith on first, and batter, Brown, hits home run inside the park. Jones fails to touch third on his way to the plate. Smith and Brown score. The defense holds the ball on third, appeals to umpire, and Jones is out. Smith's and Brown's runs count.

Approved Ruling: Two out, Jones on second, Smith on first and batter, Brown, hits home run inside the park. All three runs cross the plate. But Jones missed third base, and on appeal is declared out. Three outs. Smith's and Brown's runs are voided. No score on the play.

Approved Ruling: One out, Jones on third, Smith on second. Batter Brown flies out to center. Two out. Jones scores after catch and Smith scores on bad throw to plate. But Jones, on appeal, is adjudged to have left third before the catch and is out. Three outs. No runs.

Approved Ruling: Two out, bases full, batter hits home run over fence. Batter, on appeal, is declared out for missing first base. Three outs. No run counts.

Here is a general statement that covers:

When a runner misses a base and a fielder holds the ball on a missed base, or on the base originally occupied by the runner if a fly ball is caught, and appeals for the umpire's decision, the runner is out when the umpire sustains the appeal; all runners may score if possible, except that with two out the runner is out at the moment he misses the bag, if an appeal is sustained as applied to the following runners.

Approved Ruling: One out, Jones on third, Smith on first, and Brown flies out to right field. Two outs. Jones tags up and scores after the catch. Smith attempted to return to first but the right fielder's throw beat him to the base. Three outs. But Jones scored before the throw to catch Smith reached first base, hence Jones' run counts. It was not a force play.

4.10 (a) A regulation game consists of nine innings, unless extended because of a tie score, or shortened (1) because the home team needs none of its half of the ninth inning or only a fraction of it, or (2) because the umpire calls the game. EXCEPTION: National Association leagues may adopt a rule providing that one or both games of a doubleheader shall be seven innings in length. In such games, any of these rules applying to the ninth inning shall apply to the seventh inning.

(b) If the score is tied after nine completed innings, play shall continue until (1) the visiting team has scored more total runs than the home team at the end of a completed inning, or (2) the home team scores the winning run in an uncompleted inning.

(c) If a game is called, it is a regulation game:
(1) If five innings have been completed;
(2) If the home team has scored more runs in four or four and a fraction half-innings than the visiting team has scored in five completed half-innings;
(3) If the home team scores one or more runs in its half of the fifth inning to tie the score.

(d) If each team has the same number of runs when the game ends, the umpire shall declare it a "Tie Game."

(e) If a game is called before it has become a regulation game, the umpire shall declare it "No Game."

(f) Rain checks will not be honored for any regulation or suspended game which has progressed to or beyond a point of play described in 4.10(c).

4.11 The score of a regulation game is the total number of runs scored by each team at the moment the game ends.

(a) The game ends when the visiting team completes its half of the ninth inning if the home team is ahead.

(b) The game ends when the ninth inning is completed, if the visiting team is ahead.

(c) If the home team scores the winning run in its half of the ninth inning (or its half of an extra inning after a tie), the game ends immediately when the winning run is scored. EXCEPTION: If the last batter in a game hits a home run out of the playing field, the batter-runner and all runners on base are permitted to score, in accordance with the base-running rules, and the game ends when the batter-runner touches home plate.

APPROVED RULING: The batter hits a home run out of the playing field to win the game in the last half of the ninth or an extra inning, but is called out for passing a preceding runner. The game ends immediately when the winning run is scored.

(d) A called game ends at the moment the umpire terminates play. EXCEPTION: If the game is called while an inning is in progress and before it is completed, the game becomes a SUSPENDED game in each of the following situations:
(1) The visiting team has scored one or more runs to tie the score and the home team has not scored;
(2) The visiting team has scored one or more runs to take the lead and the home team has not tied the score or retaken the lead.

National Association Leagues may also adopt the following rules for suspended games in addition to 4.11 (d) (1) & (2) above. (if adopted by a National Association League, Rule 4.10 (c), (d) & (e) would not apply to their games):
(3) The game has not become a regulation game (4½ innings with the home team ahead, or 5 innings with the visiting club ahead or tied).
(4) Any regulation game tied at the point play is stopped because of weather, curfew or other reason.
(5) If a game is suspended before it becomes a regulation game, and is continued prior to another regularly scheduled game, the regularly scheduled game will be limited to seven innings.
(6) If a game is suspended after it is a regulation game, and is continued prior to another regularly scheduled game, the regularly scheduled game will be a nine inning game.

EXCEPTION: The above sections (3), (4), (5) & (6) will not apply to the last scheduled game between the two teams during the championship season, or League Playoffs. Any suspended game not completed prior to the last scheduled game between the two teams during the championship season, will become a called game.

4.12 SUSPENDED GAMES.

(a) A league shall adopt the following rules providing for completion at a future date of games terminated for any of the following reasons:
(1) A curfew imposed by law;
(2) A time limit permissible under league rules;
(3) Light failure or malfunction of a mechanical field device under control of the home club. (Mechanical field device shall include automatic tarpaulin or water removal equipment).
(4) Darkness, when a law prevents the lights from being turned on.
(5) Weather, if the game is called while an inning is in progress and before it is completed, and one of the following situations prevails:
(i) The visiting team has scored one or more runs to tie the score, and the home team has not scored.
(ii) The visiting team has scored one or more runs to take the lead, and the home team has not tied the score or retaken the lead.

(b) Such games shall be known as suspended games. No game called because of a curfew, weather, or a time limit shall be a suspended game unless it has progressed far enough to have been a regulation game under the provisions of Rule 4.10. A game called under the provisions of 4.12(a), (3) or (4) shall be a suspended game at any time after it starts.

NOTE: Weather and similar conditions—4.12 (a) (1 through 5)—shall take precedence in determining whether a called game shall be a suspended game. A game can only be considered a suspended game if stopped for any of the five (5) reasons specified in Section (a). Any regulation game called due to weather with the score tied(unless situation outlined in 4.12 (a) (5) (i) prevails) is a tie game and must be replayed in its entirety.

(c) A suspended game shall be resumed and completed as follows:
(1) Immediately preceding the next scheduled single game between the two Clubs on the same grounds; or
(2) Immediately preceding the next scheduled doubleheader between the two Clubs on the same grounds, if no single game remains on the schedule; or
(3) If suspended on the last scheduled date between the two Clubs in that city, transferred and played on the grounds of the opposing Club, if possible;
(i) Immediately preceding the next scheduled single game, or
(ii) Immediately preceding the next scheduled doubleheader, if no single game remains on the schedule.
(4) If a suspended game has not been resumed and completed on the last date scheduled for the two Clubs, it shall be a called game.

(d) A suspended game shall be resumed at the exact point of suspension of the original game. The completion of a suspended game is a continuation of the original game. The lineup and batting order of both teams shall be exactly the same as the lineup and batting order at the moment of suspension, subject to the rules governing substitution. Any player may be replaced by a player who had not been in the game prior to the suspension. No player removed before the suspension may be returned to the lineup.

A player who was not with the Club when the game was suspended may be used as a substitute, even if he has taken the place of a player no longer with the Club who would not have been eligible because he had been removed from the lineup before the game was suspended.

If immediately prior to the call of a suspended game, a substitute pitcher has been announced but has not retired the side or pitched until the batter becomes a baserunner, such pitcher, when the suspended game is later resumed may, but is not required to start the resumed portion of the game. However, if he does not start he will be considered as having been substituted for and may not be used in that game.

(e) Rain checks will not be honored for any regulation or suspended game which has progressed to or beyond a point of play described in 4.10 (c).

4.13 RULES GOVERNING DOUBLEHEADERS.

(a) (1) Only two championship games shall be played on one date. Completion of a suspended game shall not violate this rule.

(2) If two games are scheduled to be played for one admission on one date, the first game shall be the regularly scheduled game for that date.

(b) After the start of the first game of a doubleheader, that game shall be completed before the second game of the doubleheader shall begin.

(c) The second game of a doubleheader shall start twenty minutes after the first game is completed, unless a longer interval (not to exceed thirty minutes) is declared by the umpire-in-chief and announced to the opposing managers at the end of the first game. EXCEPTION: If the league president has approved a request of the home Club for a longer interval between games for some special event, the umpire-in-chief shall declare such longer interval and announce it to the opposing managers. The umpire-in-chief of the first game shall be the timekeeper controlling the interval between games.

(d) The umpire shall start the second game of a doubleheader, if at all possible, and play shall continue as long as ground conditions, local time restrictions, or weather permit.

(e) When a regularly scheduled doubleheader is delayed in starting for any cause, any game that is started is the first game of the doubleheader.

(f) When a rescheduled game is part of a doubleheader the rescheduled game shall be the second game, and the first game shall be the regularly scheduled game for that date.

4.14 The umpire-in-chief shall order the playing field lights turned on whenever in his opinion darkness makes further play in daylight hazardous.

4.15 A game may be forfeited to the opposing team when a team—

(a) Fails to appear upon the field, or being upon the field, refuses to start play within five minutes after the umpire has called "Play" at the appointed hour for beginning the game, unless such delayed appearance is, in the umpire's judgment, unavoidable;

(b) Employs tactics palpably designed to delay or shorten the game;

(c) Refuses to continue play during a game unless the game has been suspended or terminated by the umpire;

(d) Fails to resume play, after a suspension, within one minute after the umpire has called "Play;"

(e) After warning by the umpire, wilfully and persistently violates any rules of the game;

(f) Fails to obey within a reasonable time the umpire's order for removal of a player from the game;

(g) Fails to appear for the second game of a doubleheader within twenty minutes after the close of the first game unless the umpire-in-chief of the first game shall have extended the time of the intermission.

4.16 A game shall be forfeited to the visiting team if, after it has been suspended, the order of the umpire to groundskeepers respecting preparation of the field for resumption of play are not complied with.

4.17 A game shall be forfeited to the opposing team when a team is unable or refuses to place nine players on the field.

4.18 If the umpire declares a game forfeited he shall transmit a written report to the league president within twenty-four hours thereafter, but failure of such transmittal shall not effect the forfeiture.

4.19 PROTESTING GAMES. Each league shall adopt rules governing procedure for protesting a game, when a manager claims that an umpire's decision is in violation of these rules. No protest shall ever be permitted on judgment decisions by the umpire. In all protested games, the decision of the league president shall be final.

Even if it is held that the protested decision violated the rules, no replay of the game will be ordered unless in the opinion of the league president the violation adversely affected the protesting team's chances of winning the game.

Whenever a manager protests a game because of alleged misapplication of the rules the protest will not be recognized unless the umpires are notified at the time the play under protest occurs and before the next pitch is made or a runner is retired. A protest arising on a game-ending play may be filed until 12:00 noon the following day with the League Office.

5.00—Putting the Ball in Play; Live Ball.

5.01 At the time set for beginning the game the umpire shall call "Play."

5.02 After the umpire calls "Play" the ball is alive and in play and remains alive and in play until for legal cause, or at the umpire's call of "Time" suspending play, the ball becomes dead. While the ball is dead no player may be put out, no bases may be run and no runs may be scored, except that runners may advance one or more bases as the result of acts which occurred while the ball was alive (such as, but not limited, to a balk, an overthrow, interference, or a home run or other fair ball hit out of the playing field).

Should a ball come partially apart in a game, it is in play until the play is completed.

5.03 The pitcher shall deliver the pitch to the batter who may elect to strike the ball, or who may not offer at it, as he chooses.

5.04 The offensive team's objective is to have its batter become a runner, and its runners advance.

5.05 The defensive team's objective is to prevent offensive players from becoming runners, and to prevent their advance around the bases.

5.06 When a batter becomes a runner and touches all bases legally he shall score one run for his team.

A run legally scored cannot be nullified by subsequent action of the runner, such as but not limited to an effort to return to third base in the belief that he had left the base before a caught fly ball.

5.07 When three offensive players are legally put out, that team takes the field and the opposing team becomes the offensive team.

5.08 If a thrown ball accidently touches a base coach, or a pitched or thrown ball touches an umpire, the ball is alive and in play. However, if the coach interferes with a thrown ball, the runner is out.

5.09 The ball becomes dead and runners advance one base, or return to their bases, without liability to be put out, when—

(a) A pitched ball touches a batter, or his clothing, while in his legal batting position; runners, if forced, advance;

(b) The plate umpire interferes with the catcher's throw; runners may not advance;

NOTE: The interference shall be disregarded if the catcher's throw retires the runner.

(c) A balk is committed; runners advance (See Penalty 8.05);

(d) A ball is illegally batted; runners return;

(e) A foul ball is not caught; runners return. The umpire shall not put the ball in play until all runners have retouched their bases;

(f) A fair ball touches a runner or an umpire on fair territory before it touches an infielder including the pitcher, or touches an umpire before it has passed an infielder other than the pitcher;

If a fair ball touches an umpire working in the infield after it has bounded past, or over, the pitcher, it is a dead ball. If a batted ball is deflected by a fielder in fair territory and hits a runner or an umpire while still in flight and then caught by an infielder it shall not be a catch, but the ball shall remain in play.

If a fair ball goes through, or by, an infielder, and touches a runner immediately back of him, or touches a runner after being deflected by an infielder, the ball is in play and the umpire shall not declare the runner out. In making such decision the umpire must be convinced that the ball passed through, or by, the infielder and that no other infielder had the chance to make a play on the ball; runners advance, if forced;

(g) A pitched ball lodges in the umpire's or catcher's mask or paraphernalia, and remains out of play; runners advance one base;

If a foul tip hits the umpire and is caught by a fielder on the rebound, the ball is "dead" and the batsman cannot be called out. The same shall apply where such foul tip lodges in the umpire's mask or other paraphernalia.

If a third strike (not a foul tip) passes the catcher and hits an umpire, the ball is in play. If such ball rebounds and is caught by a fielder before it touches the ground, the batsman is not out on such a catch, but the ball remains in play and the batsman may be retired at first base, or touched with the ball for the out.

If a pitched ball lodges in the umpire's or catcher's mask or paraphernalia, and remains out of play, on the third strike or fourth ball, then the batter is entitled to first base and all runners advance one base. If the count on the batter is less than three balls, runners advance one base.

(h) Any legal pitch touches a runner trying to score; runners advance.

5.10 The ball becomes dead when an umpire calls "Time." The umpire-in-chief shall call "Time"—

(a) When in his judgment weather, darkness or similiar conditions make immedate further play impossible;

(b) When light failure makes it difficult or impossible for the umpires to follow the play;

NOTE: A league may adopt its own regulations governing games interrupted by light failure.

(c) When an accident incapacitates a player or an umpire;

(1) If an accident to a runner is such as to prevent him from proceeding to a base to which he is entitled, as on a home run hit out of the playing field, or an award of one or more bases, a substitute runner shall be permitted to complete the play.

(d) When a manager requests "Time" for a substitution, or for a conference with one of his players;

(e) When the umpire wishes to examine the ball, to consult with either manager, or for any similar cause;

(f) When a fielder, after catching a fly ball, falls into a bench or stand, or falls across ropes into a crowd when spectators are on the field. As pertains to runners, the provisions of 7.04 (c) shall prevail;

If a fielder after making a catch steps into a bench, but does not fall, the ball is in play and runners may advance at their own peril.

(g) When an umpire orders a player or any other person removed from the playing field; and/or

(h) Except in the cases stated in paragraphs (b) and (c) (1) of this rule, no umpire shall call "Time" while a play is in progress.

5.11 After the ball is dead, play shall be resumed when the pitcher takes his place on the pitcher's plate with a new ball or the same ball in his possession and the plate umpire calls "Play." The plate umpire shall call "Play" as soon as the pitcher takes his place on his plate with the ball in his possession.

6.00—The Batter.

6.01 (a) Each player of the offensive team shall bat in the order that his name appears in his team's batting order.

(b) The first batter in each inning after the first inning shall be the player whose name follows that of the last player who legally completed his time at bat in the preceding inning.

6.02 (a) The batter shall take his position in the batter's box promptly when it is his time at bat.

(b) The batter shall not leave his position in the batter's box after the pitcher comes to Set Position, or starts his windup.

PENALTY: If the pitcher pitches, the umpire shall call "Ball" or "Strike," as the case may be.

The batter leaves the batter's box at the risk of having a strike delivered and called, unless he requests the umpire to call "Time." The batter is not at liberty to step in and out of the batter's box at will.

Once a batter has taken his position in the batter's box, he shall not be permitted to step out of the batter's box in order to use the resin or the pine tar rag, unless there is a delay in the game action or, in the judgment of the umpires, weather conditions warrant an exception.

Umpires will not call "Time" at the request of the batter or any member of his team once the pitcher has started his windup or has come to a set position even though the batter claims "dust in his eyes," "steamed glasses," "didn't get the sign" or for any other cause.

Umpires may grant a hitter's request for "Time" once he is in the batter's box, but the umpire should eliminate hitters walking out of the batter's box without reason. If umpires are not lenient, batters will understand that they are in the batter's box and they must remain there until the ball is pitched.

If pitcher delays once the batter is in his box and the umpire feels that the delay is not justified he may allow the batter to step out of the box momentarily.

If after the pitcher starts his wind-up or comes to a "set position" with a runner on, he does not go through with his pitch because the batter has stepped out of the box, it shall not be called a balk. Both the pitcher and batter have violated a rule and the umpire shall call time and both the batter and pitcher start over from "scratch."

(c) If the batter refuses to take his position in the batter's box during his time at bat, the umpire shall order the pitcher to pitch, and shall call "Strike" on each such pitch. The batter may take his proper position after any such pitch, and the regular ball and strike count shall continue, but if he does not take his proper position before three strikes are called, he shall be declared out.

6.03 The batter's legal position shall be with both feet within the batter's box.

APPROVED RULING: The lines defining the box are within the batter's box.

6.04 A batter has legally completed his time at bat when he is put out or becomes a runner.

6.05 A batter is out when—

(a) His fair or foul fly ball (other than a foul tip) is legally caught by a fielder;

(b) A third strike is legally caught by the catcher;

"Legally caught" means in the catcher's glove before the ball touches the ground. It is not legal if the ball lodges in his clothing or paraphernalia, or if it touches the umpire and is caught by the catcher on the rebound.

If a foul-tip first strikes the catcher's glove and then goes on through and is caught by both hands against his body or protector, before the ball touches the ground, it is a strike, and if third strike, batter is out. If smothered against his body or protector, it is a catch provided the ball struck the catcher's glove or hand first.

(c) A third strike is not caught by the catcher when first base is occupied before two are out;

(d) He bunts foul on third strike;

(e) An Infield Fly is declared;

(f) He attempts to hit a third strike and the ball touches him;

(g) His fair ball touches him before touching a fielder;

(h) After hitting or bunting a fair ball, his bat hits the ball a second time in fair territory. The ball is dead and no runners may advance. If the batter-runner drops his bat and the ball rolls against the bat in fair territory and, in the umpire's judgment, there was no intention to interfere with the course of the ball, the ball is alive and in play;

If a bat breaks and part of it is in fair territory and is hit by a batted ball or part of it hits a runner or fielder, play shall continue and no interference called. If batted ball hits part of broken bat in foul territory, it is a foul ball.

If a whole bat is thrown into fair territory and interferes with a defensive player attempting to make a play, interference shall be called, whether intentional or not.

In cases where the batting helmet is accidentally hit with a batted or thrown ball, the ball remains in play the same as if it had not hit the helmet.

If a batted ball strikes a batting helmet or any other object foreign to the natural ground while on foul territory, it is a foul ball and the ball is dead.

If, in the umpire's judgment, there is intent on the part of a baserunner to interfere with a batted or thrown ball by dropping the helmet or throwing it at the ball, then the runner would be out, the ball dead and runners would return to last base legally touched.

(i) After hitting or bunting a foul ball, he intentionally deflects the course of the ball in any manner while running to first base. The ball is dead and no runners may advance;

(j) After a third strike or after he hits a fair ball, he or first base is tagged before he touches first base;

(k) In running the last half of the distance from home base to first base, while the ball is being fielded to first base, he runs outside (to the right of) the three-foot line, or inside (to the left of) the foul line, and in the umpire's judgment in so doing interferes with the fielder taking the throw at first base; except that he may run outside (to the right of) the three-foot line or inside (to the left of) the foul line to avoid a fielder attempting to field a batted ball;

(l) An infielder intentionally drops a fair fly ball or line drive, with first, first and second, first and third, or first, second and third base occupied before two are out. The ball is dead and runner or runners shall return to their original base or bases;

APPROVED RULING: In this situation, the batter is not out if the infielder permits the ball to drop untouched to the ground, except when the Infield Fly rule applies.

(m)A preceding runner shall, in the umpire's judgment, intentionally interfere with a fielder who is attempting to catch a thrown ball or to throw a ball in an attempt to complete any play;

The objective of this rule is to penalize the offensive team for deliberate, unwarranted, unsportsman-like action by the runner in leaving the baseline for the obvious purpose of crashing the pivot man on a double play, rather than trying to reach the base. Obviously this is an umpire's judgment play.

(n) With two out, a runner on third base, and two strikes on the batter, the runner attempts to steal home base on a legal pitch and the ball touches the runner in the batter's strike zone. The umpire shall call "Strike Three," the batter is out and the run shall not count; before two are out, the umpire shall call "Strike Three," the ball is dead, and the run counts.

6.06 A batter is out for illegal action when—

(a) He hits a ball with one or both feet on the ground entirely outside the batter's box.

If a batter hits a ball fair or foul while out of the batter's box, he shall be called out. Umpires should pay particular attention to the position of the batter's feet if he attempts to hit the ball while he is being intentionally passed. A batter cannot jump or step out of the batter's box and hit the ball.

(b) He steps from one batter's box to the other while the pitcher is in position ready to pitch;

(c) He interferes with the catcher's fielding or throwing by stepping out of the batter's box or making any other movement that hinders the catcher's play at home base. EXCEPTION: Batter is not out if any runner attempting to advance is put out, or if runner trying to score is called out for batter's interference.

If the batter interferes with the catcher, the plate umpire shall call "interference." The batter is out and the ball dead. No player may advance on such interference (offensive interference) and all runners must return to the last base that was, in the judgment of the umpire, legally touched at the time of the interference.

If, however, the catcher makes a play and a runner attempting to advance is put out, it is to be assumed there was no actual interference and that runner is out—not the batter. Any other runners on the base at the time may advance as the ruling is that there is no actual interference if a runner is retired. In that case play proceeds just as if no violation had been called.

If a batter strikes at a ball and misses and swings so hard he carries the bat all the way around and, in the umpire's judgment, unintentionally hits the catcher or the ball in back of him on the backswing before the catcher has securely held the ball, it shall be called a strike only (not interference). The ball will be dead, however, and no runner shall advance on the play.

(d) He uses or attempts to use a bat that, in the umpire's judgment, has been altered or tampered with in such a way to improve the distance factor or cause an unusual reaction on the baseball. This includes bats that are filled, flat-surfaced, nailed, hollowed, grooved or covered with a substance such as paraffin, wax, etc.

No advancement on the bases will be allowed and any out or outs made during a play shall stand.

In addition to being called out, the player shall be ejected from the game and may be subject to additional penalties as determined by his league president.

6.07 BATTING OUT OF TURN.

(a) A batter shall be called out, on appeal, when he fails to bat in his proper turn, and another batter completes a time at bat in his place.

(1) The proper batter may take his place in the batter's box at any time before the improper batter becomes a runner or is put out, and any balls and strikes shall be counted in the proper batter's time at bat.

(b) When an improper batter becomes a runner or is put out, and the defensive team appeals to the umpire before the first pitch to the next batter of either team, or before any play or attempted play, the umpire shall (1) declare the proper batter out; and (2) nullify any advance or score made because of a ball batted by the improper batter or because of the improper batter's advance to first base on a hit, an error, a base on balls, a hit batter or otherwise.

NOTE: If a runner advances, while the improper batter is at bat, on a stolen base, balk, wild pitch or passed ball, such advance is legal.

(c) When an improper batter becomes a runner or is put out, and a pitch is made to the next batter of either team before an appeal is made, the improper batter thereby becomes the proper batter, and the results of his time at bat become legal.

(d) (1) When the proper batter is called out because he has failed to bat in turn, the next batter shall be the batter whose name follows that of the proper batter thus called out; (2) when an improper batter becomes a proper batter because no appeal is made before the next pitch, the next batter shall be the batter whose name follows that of such legalized improper batter. The instant an improper batter's actions are legalized, the batting order picks up with the name following that of the legalized improper batter.

The umpire shall not direct the attention of any person to the presence in the batter's box of an improper batter. This rule is designed to require constant vigilance by the players and managers of both teams.

There are two fundamentals to keep in mind: When a player bats out of turn, the proper batter is the player called out. If an improper batter bats and reaches base or is out and no appeal is made before a pitch to the next batter, or before any play or attempted play, that improper batter is considered to have batted in proper turn and establishes the order that is to follow.

APPROVED RULING

To illustrate various situations arising from batting out of turn, assume a first-inning batting order as follows:

Abel - Baker - Charles - Daniel - Edward - Frank - George - Hooker - Irwin.

PLAY (1). Baker bats. With the count 2 balls and 1 strike, (a) the offensive team discovers the error or (b) the defensive team appeals. RULING: In either case, Abel replaces Baker, with the count on him 2 balls and 1 strike.

PLAY (2). Baker bats and doubles. The defensive team appeals (a) immediately or (b) after a pitch to Charles. RULING: (a) Abel is called out and Baker is the proper batter; (b) Baker stays on second and Charles is the proper batter.

PLAY (3). Abel walks. Baker walks. Charles forces Baker. Edward bats in Daniel's turn. While Edward is at bat, Abel scores and Charles goes to second on a wild pitch. Edward grounds out, sending Charles to third. The defensive team appeals (a) immediately or (b) after a pitch to Daniel. RULING: (a) Abel's run counts and Charles is entitled to second base since these advances were not made because of the improper batter batting a ball or advancing to first base. Charles must return to second base because his advance to third resulted from the improper batter batting a ball. Daniel is called out, and Edward is the proper batter; (b) Abel's run counts and Charles stays on third. The proper batter is Frank.

PLAY (4). With the bases full and two out, Hooker bats in Frank's turn, and triples, scoring three runs. The defensive team appeals (a) immediately, or (b) after a pitch to George. RULING: (a) Frank is called out and no runs score. George is the proper batter to lead off the second inning; (b) Hooker stays on third and three runs score. Irwin is the proper batter.

PLAY (5). After Play (4) (b) above, George continues at bat. (a) Hooker is picked off third base for the third out, or (b) George flies out, and no appeal is made. Who is the proper leadoff batter in the second inning? RULING: (a) Irwin. He became the proper batter as soon as the first pitch to George legalized Hooker's triple; (b) Hooker. When no appeal was made, the first pitch to the leadoff batter of the opposing team legalized George's time at bat.

PLAY (6). Daniel walks and Abel comes to bat. Daniel was an improper batter, and if an appeal is made before the first pitch to Abel, Abel is out, Daniel is removed from base, and Baker is the proper batter. There is no appeal, and a pitch is made to Abel. Daniel's walk is now legalized, and Edward thereby becomes the proper batter. Edward can replace Abel at any time before Abel is put out or becomes a runner. He does not do so. Abel flies out, and Baker comes to bat. Abel was an improper batter, and if an appeal is made before the first pitch to Baker, Edward is out, and the proper batter is Frank. There is no appeal, and a pitch is made to Baker. Abel's out is now legalized, and the proper batter is Baker. Baker walks. Charles is the proper batter. Charles flies out. Now Daniel is the proper batter, but he is on second base. Who is the proper batter? RULING: The proper batter is Edward. When the proper batter is on base, he is passed over, and the following batter becomes the proper batter.

6.08 The batter becomes a runner and is entitled to first base without liability to be put out (provided he advances to and touches first base) when—

(a) Four "balls" have been called by the umpire;

A batter who is entitled to first base because of a base on balls must go to first base and touch the base before other base runners are forced to advance. This applies when bases are full and applies when a substitute runner is put into the game.

If, in advancing, the base runner thinks there is a play and he slides past the base before or after touching it he may be put out by the fielder tagging him. If he fails to touch the base to which he is entitled and attempts to advance beyond that base he may be put out by tagging him or the base he missed.

(b) He is touched by a pitched ball which he is not attempting to hit unless (1) the ball is in the strike zone when it touches the batter, or (2) the batter makes no attempt to avoid being touched by the ball.

If the ball is in the strike zone when it touches the batter, it shall be called a strike, whether or not the batter tries to avoid the ball. If the ball is outside the strike zone when it touches the batter, it shall be called a ball if he makes no attempt to avoid being touched.

APPROVED RULING: When the batter is touched by a pitched ball which does not entitle him to first base, the ball is dead and no runner may advance.

(c) The catcher or any fielder interferes with him. If a play follows the interference, the manager of the offense may advise the plate umpire that he elects to decline the interference penalty and accept the play. Such election shall be made immediately at the end of the play. However, if the batter reaches first base on a hit, an error, a base on balls, a hit batsman, or otherwise, and all other runners advance at least one base, the play proceeds without reference to the interference.

If catcher's interference is called with a play in progress, the umpire will allow the play to continue because the manager may elect to take the play. If the batter-runner missed first base, or a runner misses his next base, he shall be considered as having reached the base, as stated in Note of Rule 7.04 (d).

Examples of plays the manager might elect to take:

1. Runner on third, one out, batter hits fly ball to the outfield on which the runner scores but catcher's interference was called. The offensive manager may elect to take the run and have batter called out or have runner remain at third and batter awarded first base.

2. Runner on second base. Catcher interferes with batter as he bunts ball fairly sending runner to third base. The manager may rather have runner on third base with an out on the play than have runners on second and first.

In situations where the manager wants the "interference" penalty to apply, the following interpretation shall be made of 6.08 (c):

If the catcher (or any fielder) interferes with the batter, the batter is awarded first base. If, on such interference a runner is trying to score by a steal or squeeze from third base, the ball is dead and the runner on third scores and batter is awarded first base. If the catcher interferes with the batter with no runners trying to score from third on a squeeze or steal, then the ball is dead, batter is awarded first base and runners who are forced to advance, do advance. Runners not attempting to steal or not forced to advance remain on the base they occupied at the time of the interference.

If the catcher interferes with the batter before the pitcher delivers the ball, it shall not be considered interference on the batter under Rule 6.08 (c). In such cases, the umpire shall call "Time" and the pitcher and batter start over from "scratch."

(d) A fair ball touches an umpire or a runner on fair territory before touching a fielder.

If a fair ball touches an umpire after having passed a fielder other than the pitcher, or having touched a fielder, including the pitcher, the ball is in play.

6.09 The batter becomes a runner when—

(a) He hits a fair ball;

(b) The third strike called by the umpire is not caught, providing (1) first base is unoccupied, or (2) first base is occupied with two out;

When a batter becomes a base runner on a third strike not caught by the catcher and starts for the dugout, or his position, and then realizes his situation and attempts then to reach first base, he is not out unless he or first base is tagged before he reaches first base. If, however, he actually reaches the dugout or dugout steps, he may not then attempt to go to first base and shall be out.

(c) A fair ball, after having passed a fielder other than the pitcher, or after having been touched by a fielder, including the pitcher, shall touch an umpire or runner on fair territory;

(d) A fair ball passes over a fence or into the stands at a distance from home base of 250 feet or more. Such hit entitles the batter to a home run when he shall have touched all bases legally. A fair fly ball that passes out of the playing field at a point less than 250 feet from home base shall entitle the batter to advance to second base only;

(e) A fair ball, after touching the ground, bounds into the stands, or passes through, over or under a fence, or through or under a scoreboard, or through or under shrubbery, or vines on the fence, in which case the batter and the runners shall be entitled to advance two bases;

(f) Any fair ball which, either before or after touching the ground, passes through or under a fence, or through or under a scoreboard, or through any opening in the fence or scoreboard, or through or under shrubbery, or vines on the fence, or which sticks in a fence or scoreboard, in which case the batter and the runners shall be entitled to two bases;

(g) Any bounding fair ball is deflected by the fielder into the stands, or over or under a fence on fair or foul territory, in which case the batter and all runners shall be entitled to advance two bases;

(h) Any fair fly ball is deflected by the fielder into the stands, or over the fence into foul territory, in which case the batter shall be entitled to advance to second base; but if deflected into the stands or over the fence in fair territory, the batter shall be entitled to a home run. However, should such a fair fly be deflected at a point less than 250 feet from home plate, the batter shall be entitled to two bases only.

6.10 Any League may elect to use the Designated Hitter Rule.

(a) In the event of inter-league competition between clubs of Leagues using the Designated Hitter Rule and clubs of Leagues not using the Designated Hitter Rule, the rule will be used as follows:

1. In World Series or exhibition games, the rule will be used or not used as is the practice of the home team.
2. In All-Star games, the rule will only be used if both teams and both Leagues so agree.

(b) The Rule provides as follows:

A hitter may be designated to bat for the starting pitcher and all subsequent pitchers in any game without otherwise affecting the status of the pitcher(s) in the game. A Designated Hitter for the pitcher must be selected prior to the game and must be included in the lineup cards presented to the Umpire in Chief.

The designated hitter named in the starting lineup must come to bat at least one time, unless the opposing club changes pitchers.

It is not mandatory that a club designate a hitter for the pitcher, but failure to do so prior to the game precludes the use of a Designated Hitter for that game.

Pinch hitters for a Designated Hitter may be used. Any substitute hitter for a Designated Hitter becomes the Designated Hitter. A replaced Designated Hitter shall not re-enter the game in any capacity.

The Designated Hitter may be used defensively, continuing to bat in the same position in the batting order, but the pitcher must then bat in the place of the substituted defensive player, unless more than one substitution is made, and the manager then must designate their spots in the batting order.

A runner may be substituted for the Designated Hitter and the runner assumes the role of Designated Hitter. A Designated Hitter may not pinch run.

A Designated Hitter is "locked" into the batting order. No multiple substitutions may be made that will alter the batting rotation of the Designated Hitter.

Once the game pitcher is switched from the mound to a defensive position this move shall terminate the Designated Hitter role for the remainder of the game.

Once a pinch hitter bats for any player in the batting order and then enters the game to pitch, this move shall terminate the Designated Hitter role for the remainder of the game.

Once the game pitcher bats for the Designated Hitter this move shall terminate the Designated Hitter role for the remainder of the game. (The game pitcher may only pinch-hit for the Designated Hitter).

Once a Designated Hitter assumes a defensive position this move shall terminate the Designated Hitter role for the remainder of the game. A substitute for the Designated Hitter need not be announced until it is the Designated Hitter's turn to bat.

7.00—The Runner.

7.01 A runner acquires the right to an unoccupied base when he touches it before he is out. He is then entitled to it until he is put out, or forced to vacate it for another runner legally entitled to that base.

If a runner legally acquires title to a base, and the pitcher assumes his pitching position, the runner may not return to a previously occupied base.

7.02 In advancing, a runner shall touch first, second, third and home base in order. If forced to return, he shall retouch all bases in reverse order, unless the ball is dead under any provision of Rule 5.09. In such cases, the runner may go directly to his original base.

7.03 Two runners may not occupy a base, but if, while the ball is alive, two runners are touching a base, the following runner shall be out when tagged. The preceding runner is entitled to the base.

7.04 Each runner, other than the batter, may without liability to be put out, advance one base when—

(a) There is a balk;

(b) The batter's advance without liability to be put out forces the runner to vacate his base, or when the batter hits a fair ball that touches another runner or the umpire before such ball has been touched by, or has passed a fielder, if the runner is forced to advance;

A runner forced to advance without liability to be put out may advance past the base to which he is entitled only at his peril. If such a runner, forced to advance, is put out for the third out before a preceding runner, also forced to advance, touches home plate, the run shall score.

Play. Two out, bases full, batter walks but runner from second is overzealous and runs past third base toward home and is tagged out on a throw by the catcher. Even though two are out, the run would score on the theory that the run was forced home by the base on balls and that all the runners needed to do was proceed and touch the next base.

(c) A fielder, after catching a fly ball, falls into a bench or stand, or falls across ropes into a crowd when spectators are on the field;

A fielder or catcher may reach or step into, or go into the dugout with one or both feet to make a catch, and if he holds the ball, the catch shall be allowed. Ball is in play.

If the fielder or catcher, after having made a legal catch, should fall into a stand or among spectators or into the dugout after making a legal catch, or fall while in the dugout after making a legal catch, the ball is dead and runners advance one base without liability to be put out.

(d) While he is attempting to steal a base, the batter is interfered with by the catcher or any other fielder.

NOTE: When a runner is entitled to a base without liability to be put out, while the ball is in play, or under any rule in which the ball is in play after the runner reaches the base to which he is entitled, and the runner fails to touch the base to which he is entitled before attempting to advance to the next base, the runner shall forfeit his exemption from liability to be put out, and he may be put out by tagging the base or by tagging the runner before he returns to the missed base.

7.05 Each runner including the batter-runner may, without liability to be put out, advance—

(a) To home base, scoring a run, if a fair ball goes out of the playing field in flight and he touches all bases legally; or if a fair ball which, in the umpire's judgment, would have gone out of the playing field in flight, is deflected by the act of a fielder in throwing his glove, cap, or any article of his apparel;

(b) Three bases, if a fielder deliberately touches a fair ball with his cap, mask or any part of his uniform detached from its proper place on his person. The ball is in play and the batter may advance to home base at his peril;

(c) Three bases, if a fielder deliberately throws his glove at and touches a fair ball. The ball is in play and the batter may advance to home base at his peril;

(d) Two bases, if a fielder deliberately touches a thrown ball with his cap, mask or any part of his uniform detached from its proper place on his person. The ball is in play;

(e) Two bases, if a fielder deliberately throws his glove at and touches a thrown ball. The ball is in play;

In applying (b-c-d-e) the umpire must rule that the thrown glove or detached cap or mask has touched the ball. There is no penalty if the ball is not touched.

Under (c-e) this penalty shall not be invoked against a fielder whose glove is carried off his hand by the force of a batted or thrown ball, or when his glove flies off his hand as he makes an obvious effort to make a legitimate catch.

(f) Two bases, if a fair ball bounces or is deflected into the stands outside the first or third base foul lines; or if it goes through or under a field fence, or through or under a scoreboard, or through or under shrubbery or vines on the fence; or if it sticks in such fence, scoreboard, shrubbery or vines;

(g) Two bases when, with no spectators on the playing field, a thrown ball goes into the stands, or into a bench (whether or not the ball rebounds into the field), or over or under or through a field fence, or on a slanting part of the screen above the backstop, or remains in the meshes of a wire screen protecting spectators. The ball is dead. When such wild throw is the first play by an infielder, the umpire, in awarding such bases, shall be governed by the position of the runners at the time the ball was pitched; in all other cases the umpire shall be governed by the position of the runners at the time the wild throw was made;

APPROVED RULING: If all runners, including the batter-runner, have advanced at least one base when an infielder makes a wild throw on the first play after the pitch, the award shall be governed by the position of the runners when the wild throw was made.

In certain circumstances it is impossible to award a runner two bases. Example: Runner on first. Batter hits fly to short right. Runner holds up between first and second and batter comes around first and pulls up behind him. Ball falls safely. Outfielder, in throwing to first, throws ball into stand.

APPROVED RULING: Since no runner, when the ball is dead, may advance beyond the base to which he is entitled, the runner originally on first base goes to third base and the batter is held at second base.

The term "when the wild throw was made" means when the throw actually left the player's hand and not when the thrown ball hit the ground, passes a receiving fielder or goes out of play into the stands.

The position of the batter-runner at the time the wild throw left the thrower's hand is the key in deciding the award of bases. If the batter-runner has not reached first base, the award is two bases at the time the pitch was made for all runners. The decision as to whether the batter-runner has reached first base before the throw is a judgment call.

If an unusual play arises where a first throw by an infielder goes into stands or dugout but the batter did not become a runner (such as catcher throwing ball into stands in attempt to get runner from third trying to score on passed ball or wild pitch) award of two bases shall be from the position of the runners at the time of the throw. (For the purpose of Rule 7.05 (g) a catcher is considered an infielder.)

PLAY. Runner on first base, batter hits a ball to the shortstop, who throws to second base too late to get runner at second, and second baseman throws toward first base after batter has crossed first base. Ruling—Runner at second scores. (On this play, only if batter-runner is past first base when throw is made is he awarded third base.)

(h) One base, if a ball, pitched to the batter, or thrown by the pitcher from his position on the pitcher's plate to a base to catch a runner, goes into a stand or a bench, or over or through a field fence or backstop. The ball is dead;

APPROVED RULING: When a wild pitch or passed ball goes through or by the catcher, or deflects off the catcher, and goes directly into the dugout, stands, above the break, or any area where the ball is dead, the awarding of bases shall be one base. One base shall also be awarded if the pitcher while in contact with the rubber, throws to a base, and the throw goes directly into the stands or into any area where the ball is dead.

If, however, the pitched or thrown ball goes through or by the catcher or through the fielder, and remains on the playing field, and is subsequently kicked or deflected into the dugout, stands or other area where the ball is dead, the awarding of bases shall be two bases from position of runners at the time of the pitch or throw.

(i) One base, if the batter becomes a runner on Ball Four or Strike Three, when the pitch passes the catcher and lodges in the umpire's mask or paraphernalia.

If the batter becomes a runner on a wild pitch which entitles the runners to advance one base, the batter-runner shall be entitled to first base only.

The fact a runner is awarded a base or bases without liability to be put out does not relieve him of the responsibility to touch the base he is awarded and all intervening bases. For example: batter hits a ground ball which an infielder throws into the stands but the batter-runner missed first base. He may be called out on appeal for missing first base after the ball is put in play even though he was "awarded" second base.

If a runner is forced to return to a base after a catch, he must retouch his original base even though, because of some ground rule or other rule, he is awarded additional bases. He may retouch while the ball is dead and the award is then made from his original base.

7.06 When obstruction occurs, the umpire shall call or signal "Obstruction."

(a) If a play is being made on the obstructed runner, or if the batter-runner is obstructed before he touches first base, the ball is dead and all runners shall advance, without liability to be put out, to the bases they would have reached, in the umpire's judgment, if there had been no obstruction. The obstructed runner shall be awarded at least one base beyond the base he had last legally touched before the obstruction. Any preceding runners, forced to advance by the award of bases as the penalty for obstruction, shall advance without liability to be put out.

When a play is being made on an obstructed runner, the umpire shall signal obstruction in the same manner that he calls "Time," with both hands overhead. The ball is immediately dead when this signal is given; however, should a thrown ball be in flight before the obstruction is called by the umpire, the runners are to be awarded such bases on wild throws as they would have been awarded had no obstruction occurred. On a play where a runner was trapped between second and third and obstructed by the third baseman going into third base while the throw is in flight from the shortstop, if such throw goes into the dugout the obstructed runner is to be awarded home base. Any other runners on base in this situation would also be awarded two bases from the base they last legally touched before obstruction was called.

(b) If no play is being made on the obstructed runner, the play shall proceed until no further action is possible. The umpire shall then call "Time" and impose such penalties, if any, as in his judgment will nullify the act of obstruction.

Under 7.06 (b) when the ball is not dead on obstruction and an obstructed runner advances beyond the base which, in the umpire's judgment, he would have been awarded because of being obstructed, he does so at his own peril and may be tagged out. This is a judgment call.

NOTE: The catcher, without the ball in his possession, has no right to block the pathway of the runner attempting to score. The base line belongs to the runner and the catcher should be there only when he is fielding a ball or when he already has the ball in his hand.

7.07 If, with a runner on third base and trying to score by means of a squeeze play or a steal, the catcher or any other fielder steps on, or in front of home base without possession of the ball, or touches the batter or his bat, the pitcher shall be charged with a balk, the batter shall be awarded first base on the interference and the ball is dead.

7.08 Any runner is out when—

(a) (1) He runs more than three feet away from a direct line between bases to avoid being tagged, unless his action is to avoid interference with a fielder fielding a batted ball; or (2) after touching first base, he leaves the baseline, obviously abandoning his effort to touch the next base;

Any runner after reaching first base who leaves the baseline heading for his dugout or his position believing that there is no further play, may be declared out if the umpire judges the act of the runner to be considered abandoning his efforts to run the bases. Even though an out is called, the ball remains in play in regard to any other runner.

This rule also covers the following and similar plays: Less than two out, score tied last of ninth inning, runner on first, batter hits a ball out of park for winning run, the runner on first passes second and thinking the home run automatically wins the game, cuts across diamond toward his bench as batter-runner circles bases. In this case, the base runner would be called out "for abandoning his effort to touch the next base" and batter-runner permitted to continue around bases to make his home run valid. If there are two out, home run would not count (see Rule 7.12). This is not an appeal play.

PLAY. Runner believing he is called out on a tag at first or third base starts for the dugout and progresses a reasonable distance still indicating by his actions that he is out, shall be declared out for abandoning the bases.

In the above two plays the runners are considered actually abandoning their base paths and are treated differently than the batter who struck out as described. APPROVED RULING OF 7.08 (a).

APPROVED RULING: When a batter becomes a runner on third strike not caught, and starts for his bench or position, he may advance to first base at any time before he enters the bench. To put him out, the defense must tag him or first base before he touches first base.

(b) He intentionally interferes with a thrown ball; or hinders a fielder attempting to make a play on a batted ball;

A runner who is adjudged to have hindered a fielder who is attempting to make a play on a batted ball is out whether it was intentional or not.

If, however, the runner has contact with a legally occupied base when he hinders the fielder, he shall not be called out unless, in the umpire's judgment, such hindrance, whether it occurs on fair or foul territory, is intentional. If the umpire declares the hindrance intentional, the following penalty shall apply: With less than two out, the umpire shall declare both the runner and batter out. With two out, the umpire shall declare the batter out.

If, in a run-down between third base and home plate, the succeeding runner has advanced and is standing on third base when the runner in a run-down is called out for offensive interference, the umpire shall send the runner standing on third base back to second base. This same principle applies if there is a run-down between second and third base and succeeding runner has reached second (the reasoning is that no runner shall advance on an interference play and a runner is considered to occupy a base until he legally has reached the next succeeding base).

(c) He is tagged, when the ball is alive, while off his base. EXCEPTION: A batter-runner cannot be tagged out after overrunning or oversliding first base if he returns immediately to the base;

APPROVED RULING: (1) If the impact of a runner breaks a base loose from its position, no play can be made on that runner at that base if he had reached the base safely.

APPROVED RULING: (2) If a base is dislodged from its position during a play, any following runner on the same play shall be considered as touching or occupying the base if, in the umpire's judgment, he touches or occupies the point marked by the dislodged bag.

(d) He fails to retouch his base after a fair or foul ball is legally caught before he, or his base, is tagged by a fielder. He shall not be called out for failure to retouch his base after the first following pitch, or any play or attempted play. This is an appeal play;

Runners need not "tag up" on a foul tip. They may steal on a foul tip. If a so-called tip is not caught, it becomes an ordinary foul. Runners then return to their bases.

(e) He fails to reach the next base before a fielder tags him or the base, after he has been forced to advance by reason of the batter becoming a runner. However, if a following runner is put out on a force play, the force is removed and the runner must be tagged to be put out. The force is removed as soon as the runner touches the base to which he is forced to advance, and if he overslides or overruns the base, the runner must be tagged to be put out. However, if the forced runner, after touching the next base, retreats for any reason towards the base he had last occupied, the force play is reinstated, and he can again be put out if the defense tags the base to which he is forced;

PLAY. Runner on first and three balls on batter: Runner steals on the next pitch, which is fourth ball, but after having touched second he overslides or overruns that base. Catcher's throw catches him before he can return. Ruling is that runner is out. (Force out is removed.)

Oversliding and overrunning situations arise at bases other than first base. For instance, before two are out, and runners on first and second, or first, second and third, the ball is hit to an infielder who tries for the double play. The runner on first beats the throw to second base but overslides the base. The relay is made to first base and the batter-runner is out. The first baseman, seeing the runner at second base off the bag, makes the return throw to second and the runner is tagged off the base. Meanwhile runners have crossed the plate. The question is: Is this a force play? Was the force removed when the batter-runner was out at first base? Do the runs that crossed the plate during this play and before the third out was made when the runner was tagged at second, count? Answer: The runs score. It is not a force play. It is a tag play.

(f) He is touched by a fair ball in fair territory before the ball has touched or passed an infielder. The ball is dead and no runner may score, nor runners advance, except runners forced to advance. EXCEPTION: If a runner is touching his base when touched by an Infield Fly, he is not out, although the batter is out;

If two runners are touched by the same fair ball, only the first one is out because the ball is instantly dead.

If runner is touched by an Infield Fly when he is not touching his base, both runner and batter are out.

(g) He attempts to score on a play in which the batter interferes with the play at home base before two are out. With two out, the interference puts the batter out and no score counts;

(h) He passes a preceding runner before such runner is out;

(i) After he has acquired legal possession of a base, he runs the bases in reverse order for the purpose of confusing the defense or making a travesty of the game. The umpire shall immediately call "Time" and declare the runner out;

If a runner touches an unoccupied base and then thinks the ball was caught or is decoyed into returning to the base he last touched, he may be put out running back to that base, but if he reaches the previously occupied base safely he cannot be put out while in contact with that base.

(j) He fails to return at once to first base after overrunning or oversliding that base. If he attempts to run to second he is out when tagged. If, after overrunning or oversliding first base he starts toward the dugout, or toward his position, and fails to return to first base at once, he is out, on appeal, when he or the base is tagged;

Runner who touches first base in overrunning and is declared safe by the umpire has, within the intent of Rule 4.09 (a) "reached first base" and any run which scores on such a play counts, even though the runner subsequently becomes the third out for failure to return "at once," as covered in Rule 7.08 (j).

(k) In running or sliding for home base, he fails to touch home base and makes no attempt to return to the base, when a fielder holds the ball in his hand, while touching home base, and appeals to the umpire for the decision.

This rule applies only where runner is on his way to the bench and the catcher would be required to chase him. It does not apply to the ordinary play where the runner misses the plate and then immediately makes an effort to touch the plate before being tagged. In that case, runner must be tagged.

7.09 It is interference by a batter or a runner when—

(a) After a third strike he hinders the catcher in his attempt to field the ball;

(b) After hitting or bunting a fair ball, his bat hits the ball a second time in fair territory. The ball is dead and no runners may advance. If the batter-runner drops his bat and the ball rolls against the bat in fair territory and, in the umpire's judgment, there was no intention to interfere with the course of the ball, the ball is alive and in play;

(c) He intentionally deflects the course of a foul ball in any manner;

(d) Before two are out and a runner on third base, the batter hinders a fielder in making a play at home base; the runner is out;

(e) Any member or members of the offensive team stand or gather around any base to which a runner is advancing, to confuse, hinder or add to the difficulty of the fielders. Such runner shall be declared out for the interference of his teammate or teammates;

(f) Any batter or runner who has just been put out hinders or impedes any following play being made on a runner. Such runner shall be declared out for the interference of his teammate;

If the batter or a runner continues to advance after he has been put out, he shall not by that act alone be considered as confusing, hindering or impeding the fielders.

(g) If, in the judgment of the umpire, a base runner wilfully and deliberately interferes with a batted ball or a fielder in the act of fielding a batted ball with the obvious intent to break up a double play, the ball is dead. The umpire shall call the runner out for interference and also call out the batter-runner because of the action of his teammate. In no event may bases be run or runs scored because of such action by a runner.

(h) If, in the judgment of the umpire, a batter-runner wilfully and deliberately interferes with a batted ball or a fielder in the act of fielding a batted ball, with the obvious intent to break up a double play, the ball is dead; the umpire shall call the batter-runner out for interference and shall also call out the runner who had advanced closest to the home plate regardless where the double play might have been possible. In no event shall bases be run because of such interference.

(i) In the judgment of the umpire, the base coach at third base, or first base, by touching or holding the runner, physically assists him in returning to or leaving third base or first base.

(j) With a runner on third base, the base coach leaves his box and acts in any manner to draw a throw by a fielder;

(k) In running the last half of the distance from home base to first base while the ball is being fielded to first base, he runs outside (to the right of) the three-foot line, or inside (to the left of) the foul line and, in the umpire's judgment, interferes with the fielder taking the throw at first base, or attempting to field a batted ball;

The lines marking the three foot lane are a part of that "lane" but the interpretation to be made is that a runner is required to have both feet within the three foot "lane" or on the lines marking the "lane."

(l) He fails to avoid a fielder who is attempting to field a batted ball, or intentionally interferes with a thrown ball, provided that if two or more fielders attempt to field a batted ball, and the runner comes in contact with one or more of them, the umpire shall determine which fielder is entitled to the benefit of this rule, and shall not declare the runner out for coming in contact with a fielder other than the one the umpire determines to be entitled to field such a ball;

When a catcher and batter-runner going to first base have contact when the catcher is fielding the ball, there is generally no violation and nothing should be called. "Obstruction" by a fielder attempting to field a ball should be called only in very flagrant and violent cases because the rules give him the right of way, but of course such "right of way" is not a license to, for example, intentionally trip a runner even though fielding the ball. If the catcher is fielding the ball and the first baseman or pitcher obstructs a runner going to first base "obstruction" shall be called and the base runner awarded first base.

(m) A fair ball touches him on fair territory before touching a fielder. If a fair ball goes through, or by, an infielder, and touches a runner immediately back of him, or touches the runner after having been deflected by a fielder, the umpire shall not declare the runner out for being touched by a batted ball. In making such decision the umpire must be convinced that the ball passed through, or by, the fielder, and that no other infielder had the chance to make a play on the ball. If, in the judgment of the umpire, the runner deliberately and intentionally kicks such a batted ball on which the infielder has missed a play, then the runner shall be called out for interference.

PENALTY FOR INTERFERENCE: The runner is out and the ball is dead.

7.10 Any runner shall be called out, on appeal, when—

(a) After a fly ball is caught, he fails to retouch his original base before he or his original base is tagged;

"Retouch," in this rule, means to tag up and start from a contact with the base after the ball is caught. A runner is not permitted to take a flying start from a position in back of his base.

(b) With the ball in play, while advancing or returning to a base, he fails to touch each base in order before he, or a missed base, is tagged.

APPROVED RULING: (1) No runner may return to touch a missed base after a following runner has scored. (2) When the ball is dead, no runner may return to touch a missed base or one he has left after he has advanced to and touched a base beyond the missed base.

PLAY. (a) Batter hits ball out of park or ground rule double and misses first base (ball is dead)—he may return to first base to correct his mistake before he touches second but if he touches second he may not return to first and if defensive team appeals he is declared out at first.

PLAY. (b) Batter hits ball to shortstop who throws wild into stand (ball is dead)—batter-runner misses first base but is awarded second base on the overthrow. Even though the umpire has awarded the runner second base on the overthrow, the runner must touch first base before he proceeds to second base.

These are appeal plays.

(c) He overruns or overslides first base and fails to return to the base immediately, and he or the base is tagged;

(d) He fails to touch home base and makes no attempt to return to that base, and home base is tagged.

Any appeal under this rule must be made before the next pitch, or any play or attempted play. If the violation occurs during a play which ends a half-inning, the appeal must be made before the defensive team leaves the field.

An appeal is not to be interpreted as a play or an attempted play.

Successive appeals may not be made on a runner at the same base. If the defensive team on its first appeal errs, a request for a second appeal on the same runner at the same base shall not be allowed by the umpire. (Intended meaning of the word "err" is that the defensive team in making an appeal threw the ball out of play. For example, if the pitcher threw to first base to appeal and threw the ball into the stands, no second appeal would be allowed.)

Appeal plays may require an umpire to recognize an apparent "fourth out." If the third out is made during a play in which an appeal play is sustained on another runner, the appeal play decision takes precedence in determining the out. If there is more than one appeal during a play that ends a half-inning, the defense may elect to take the out that gives it the advantage. For the purpose of this rule, the defensive team has "left the field" when the pitcher and all infielders have left fair territory on their way to the bench or clubhouse.

If two runners arrive at home base about the same time and the first runner misses home plate but a second runner legally touches the plate, the first runner will be called out on appeal. If there are two out, and the first runner is tagged out on his attempt to come back and touch the base or is called out on appeal, then he shall be considered as having been put out before the second runner scored and being the third out. Second runner's run shall not count, as provided in Rule 7.12.

If a pitcher balks when making an appeal, such act shall be a play. An appeal should be clearly intended as an appeal, either by a verbal request by the player or an act that unmistakably indicates an appeal to the umpire. A player, inadvertently stepping on the base with a ball in his hand, would not constitute an appeal. Time is not out when an appeal is being made.

7.11 The players, coaches or any member of an offensive team shall vacate any space (including both dugouts) needed by a fielder who is attempting to field a batted or thrown ball.

PENALTY: Interference shall be called and the batter or runner on whom the play is being made shall be declared out.

7.12 Unless two are out, the status of a following runner is not affected by a preceding runner's failure to touch or retouch a base. If, upon appeal, the preceding runner is the third out, no runners following him shall score. If such third out is the result of a force play, neither preceding nor following runners shall score.

8.00—The Pitcher.

8.01 Legal pitching delivery. There are two legal pitching positions, the Windup Position and the Set Position, and either position may be used at any time.

Pitchers shall take signs from the catcher while standing on the rubber.

Pitchers may disengage the rubber after taking their signs but may not step quickly onto the rubber and pitch. This may be judged a quick pitch by the umpire. When the pitcher disengages the rubber, he must drop his hands to his sides.

Pitchers will not be allowed to disengage the rubber after taking each sign.

(a) The Windup Position. The pitcher shall stand facing the batter, his entire pivot foot on, or in front of and touching and not off the end of the pitcher's plate, and the other foot free. From this position any natural movement associated with his delivery of the ball to the batter commits him to the pitch without interruption or alteration. He shall not raise either foot from the ground, except that in his actual delivery of the ball to the batter, he may take one step backward, and one step forward with his free foot.

When a pitcher holds the ball with both hands in front of his body, with his entire pivot foot on, or in front of and touching but not off the end of the pitcher's plate, and his other foot free, he will be considered in the Windup Position.

The pitcher may have one foot, not the pivot foot, off the rubber and any distance he may desire back of a line which is an extension to the back edge of the pitcher's plate, but not at either side of the pitcher's plate.

With his "free" foot the pitcher may take one step backward and one step forward, but under no circumstances, to either side, that is to either the first base or third base side of the pitcher's rubber.

If a pitcher holds the ball with both hands in front of his body, with his entire pivot foot on or in front of and touching but not off the end of the pitcher's plate, and his other foot free, he will be considered in a windup position.

From this position he may:

(1) deliver the ball to the batter, or

(2) step and throw to a base in an attempt to pick off a runner, or

(3) disengage the rubber (if he does he must drop his hands to his sides).

In disengaging the rubber the pitcher must step off with his pivot foot and not his free foot first.

He may not go into a set or stretch position—if he does it is a balk.

(b) The Set Position.

Preparatory to coming to a set position, the pitcher shall have one hand by his side.

Set Position is assumed by the pitcher when he stands facing the batter with his entire pivot foot on, and parallel to, the pitcher's plate, or in front of, parallel to and in contact with, the pitcher's plate. The non pivot foot must be on the ground in front of the pitcher's plate. The pitcher must hold the ball in both hands in front of his body and come to a single complete and discernible stop before throwing the ball. A complete stop shall not be construed as occuring because of a change in direction of the hands and arms.

From such Set Position he must deliver the ball to the batter, throw to a base or step backward off the pitcher's plate with his pivot foot.

Before assuming Set Position, the pitcher may elect to make any natural preliminary motion such as that known as "the stretch." But if he so elects, he shall come to a Set Position before delivering the ball to the batter. After assuming Set Position, any natural motion associated with his delivery of the ball to the batter commits him to the pitch without alteration or interruption.

The pitcher, following his stretch, must (a) hold the ball in both hands in front of his body and (b) come to a complete and discernible stop, with both feet on the ground. This must be enforced. Umpires should watch this closely, and should immediately call a "balk" for any violation.

(c) At any time during the pitcher's preliminary movements and until his natural pitching motion commits him to the pitch, he may throw to any base provided he steps directly toward such base before making the throw.

The pitcher shall step "ahead of the throw." A snap throw followed by the step directly toward the base is a balk.

(d) If the pitcher makes an illegal pitch with the bases unoccupied, it shall be called a ball unless the batter reaches first base on a hit, an error, a base on balls, a hit batter or otherwise.

A ball which slips out of a pitcher's hand and crosses the foul line shall be called a ball; otherwise it will be called no pitch. This would be a balk with men on base.

(e) If the pitcher removes his pivot foot from contact with the pitcher's plate by stepping backward with that foot, he thereby becomes an infielder and if he makes a wild throw from that position, it shall be considered the same as a wild throw by any other infielder.

The pitcher, while off the rubber, may throw to any base. If he makes a wild throw, such throw is the throw of an infielder and what follows is governed by the rules covering a ball thrown by a fielder.

8.02 The pitcher shall not—

(a) (1) Bring his pitching hand in contact with his mouth or lips while in the 18-foot circle surrounding the pitching rubber. EXCEPTION: Provided it is agreed to by both managers, the umpire, prior to the start of a game played in cold weather, may permit the pitcher to blow on his hand.

PENALTY: For violation of this part of this rule the umpires shall immediately call a ball. However, if the pitch is made and a batter reaches first base on a hit, an error, a hit batsman or otherwise, and no other runner is put out before advancing at least one base, the play shall proceed without reference to the violation. Repeated offenders shall be subject to a fine by the league president.

(2) Apply a foreign substance of any kind to the ball;

(3) expectorate on the ball, either hand or his glove;

(4) rub the ball on his glove, person or clothing;

(5) deface the ball in any manner; or

(6) deliver what is called the "shine" ball, "spit" ball, "mud" ball or "emery" ball. The pitcher, of course, is allowed to rub the ball between his bare hands.

PENALTY: For violation of any part of this rule 8.02 (a) (2 to 6) the umpire shall:

(a) Call the pitch a ball, warn the pitcher and have announced on the public address system the reason for the action.

(b) In the case of a second offense by the same pitcher in the same game, the pitcher shall be disqualified from the game.

(c) If a play follows the violation called by the umpire, the manager of the offense may advise the plate umpire that he elects to accept the play. Such election shall be made immediately at the end of the play. However, if the batter reaches first base on a hit, an error, a base on balls, a hit batsman, or otherwise, and no other runner is put out before advancing at least one base, the play shall proceed without reference to the violation.

(d) Even though the offense elects to take the play, the violation shall be recognized and the penalties in (a) and (b) will still be in effect.

(e) The umpire shall be sole judge on whether any portion of this rule has been violated.

All umpires shall carry with them one official rosin bag. The umpire-in-chief is responsible for placing the rosin bag on the ground back of the pitcher's plate. If at any time the ball hits the rosin bag it is in play. In the case of rain or wet field, the umpire may instruct the pitcher to carry the rosin bag in his hip pocket. A pitcher may use the rosin bag for the purpose of applying rosin to his bare hand or hands. Neither the pitcher nor any other player shall dust the ball with the rosin bag; neither shall the pitcher nor any other player be permitted to apply rosin from the bag to his glove or dust any part of his uniform with the rosin bag.

(b) Have on his person, or in his possession, any foreign substance. For such infraction of this section (b) the penalty shall be immediate ejection from the game.

(c) Intentionally delay the game by throwing the ball to players other than the catcher, when the batter is in position, except in an attempt to retire a runner.

PENALTY: If, after warning by the umpire, such delaying action is repeated, the pitcher shall be removed from the game.

(d) Intentionally Pitch at the Batter.

If, in the umpire's judgment, such a violation occurs, the umpire may elect either to:

1. Expel the pitcher, or the manager and the pitcher, from the game, or

2. may warn the pitcher and the manager of both teams that another such pitch will result in the immediate expulsion of that pitcher (or a replacement) and the manager.

If, in the umpire's judgment, circumstances warrant, both teams may be officially "warned" prior to the game or at any time during the game.

(League Presidents may take additional action under authority provided in Rule 9.05)

To pitch at a batter's head is unsportsmanlike and highly dangerous. It should be—and is—condemned by everybody. Umpires should act without hesitation in enforcement of this rule.

8.03 When a pitcher takes his postion at the beginning of each inning, or when he relieves another pitcher, he shall be permitted to pitch not to exceed eight preparatory pitches to his catcher during which play shall be suspended. A league by its own action may limit the number of preparatory pitches to less than eight preparatory pitches. Such preparatory pitches shall not consume more than one minute of time. If a sudden emergency causes a pitcher to be summoned into the game without any opportunity to warm up, the umpire-in-chief shall allow him as many pitches as the umpire deems necessary.

8.04 When the bases are unoccupied, the pitcher shall deliver the ball to the batter within 20 seconds after he receives the ball. Each time the pitcher delays the game by violating this rule, the umpire shall call "Ball."

The intent of this rule is to avoid unnecessary delays. The umpire shall insist that the catcher return the ball promptly to the pitcher, and that the pitcher take his position on the rubber promptly. Obvious delay by the pitcher should instantly be penalized by the umpire.

8.05 If there is a runner, or runners, it is a balk when—

(a) The pitcher, while touching his plate, makes any motion naturally associated with his pitch and fails to make such delivery;

If a lefthanded or righthanded pitcher swings his free foot past the back edge of the pitcher's rubber, he is required to pitch to the batter except to throw to second base on a pick-off play.

(b) The pitcher, while touching his plate, feints a throw to first base and fails to complete the throw;

(c) The pitcher, while touching his plate, fails to step directly toward a base before throwing to that base;

Requires the pitcher, while touching his plate, to step directly toward a base before throwing to that base. If a pitcher turns or spins off of his free foot without actually stepping or if he turns his body and throws before stepping, it is a balk.

A pitcher is to step directly toward a base before throwing to that base but is not required to throw (except to first base only) because he steps. It is possible, with runners on first and third, for the pitcher to step toward third and not throw, merely to bluff the runner back to third; then seeing the runner on first start for second, turn and step toward and throw to first base. This is legal. However, if, with runners on first and third, the pitcher, while in contact with the rubber, steps toward third and then immediately and in practically the same motion "wheels" and throws to first base, it is obviously an attempt to deceive the runner at first base, and in such a move it is practically impossible to step directly toward first base before the throw to first base, and such a move shall be called a balk. Of course, if the pitcher steps off the rubber and then makes such a move, it is not a balk.

(d) The pitcher, while touching his plate, throws, or feints a throw to an unoccupied base, except for the purpose of making a play;

(e) The pitcher makes an illegal pitch;

A quick pitch is an illegal pitch. Umpires will judge a quick pitch as one delivered before the batter is reasonably set in the batter's box. With runners on base the penalty is a balk; with no runners on base, it is a ball. The quick pitch is dangerous and should not be permitted.

(f) The pitcher delivers the ball to the batter while he is not facing the batter;

(g) The pitcher makes any motion naturally associated with his pitch while he is not touching the pitcher's plate;

(h) The pitcher unnecessarily delays the game;

(i) The pitcher, without having the ball, stands on or astride the pitcher's plate or while off the plate, he feints a pitch;

(j) The pitcher, after coming to a legal pitching position, removes one hand from the ball other than in an actual pitch, or in throwing to a base;

(k) The pitcher, while touching the plate, accidentally or intentionally drops the ball;

(l) The pitcher, while giving an intentional base on balls, pitches when the catcher is not in the catcher's box;

(m) The pitcher delivers the pitch from Set Position without coming to a stop.

PENALTY: The ball is dead, and each runner shall advance one base without liability to be put out, unless the batter reaches first on a hit, an error, a base on balls, a hit batter, or otherwise, and all other runners advance at least one base, in which case the play proceeds without reference to the balk.

APPROVED RULING: In cases where a pitcher balks and throws wild, either to a base or to home plate, a runner or runners may advance beyond the base to which he is entitled at his own risk.

APPROVED RULING: A runner who misses the first base to which he is advancing and who is called out on appeal shall be considered as having advanced one base for the purpose of this rule.

Umpires should bear in mind that the purpose of the balk rule is to prevent the pitcher from deliberately deceiving the base runner. If there is doubt in the umpire's mind, the "intent" of the pitcher should govern. However, certain specifics should be borne in mind:

(a) Straddling the pitcher's rubber without the ball is to be interpreted as intent to deceive and ruled a balk.

(b) With a runner on first base the pitcher may make a complete turn, without hesitating toward first, and throw to second. This is not to be interpreted as throwing to an unoccupied base.

8.06 A professional league shall adopt the following rule pertaining to the visit of the manager or coach to the pitcher:

(a) This rule limits the number of trips a manager or coach may make to any one pitcher in any one inning; (b) A second trip to the same pitcher in the same inning will cause this pitcher's automatic removal; (c) The manager or coach is prohibited from making a second visit to the mound while the same batter is at bat, but (d) if a pinch-hitter is substituted for this batter, the manager or coach may make a second visit to the mound, but must remove the pitcher.

A manager or coach is considered to have concluded his visit to the mound when he leaves the 18-foot circle surrounding the pitcher's rubber.

If the manager or coach goes to the catcher or infielder and that player then goes to the mound or the pitcher comes to him at his position before there is an intervening play (a pitch or other play) that will be the same as the manager or coach going to the mound.

Any attempt to evade or circumvent this rule by the manager or coach going to the catcher or an infielder and then that player going to the mound to confer with the pitcher shall constitute a trip to the mound.

If the coach goes to the mound and removes a pitcher and then the manager goes to the mound to talk with the new pitcher, that will constitute one trip to that new pitcher that inning.

In a case where a manager has made his first trip to the mound and then returns the second time to the mound in the same inning with the same pitcher in the game and the same batter at bat, after being warned by the umpire that he cannot return to the mound, the manager shall be removed from the game and the pitcher required to pitch to the batter until he is retired or gets on base. After the batter is retired, or becomes a base runner, then this pitcher must be removed from the game. The manager should be notified that his pitcher will be removed from the game after he pitches to one hitter, so he can have a substitute pitcher warmed up.

The substitute pitcher will be allowed eight preparatory pitches or more if in the umpire's judgment circumstances justify.

9.00—The Umpire

9.01 (a) The league president shall appoint one or more umpires to officiate at each league championship game. The umpires shall be responsible for the conduct of the game in accordance with these official rules and for maintaining discipline and order on the playing field during the game.

(b) Each umpire is the representative of the league and of professional baseball, and is authorized and required to enforce all of these rules. Each umpire has authority to order a player, coach, manager or club officer or employee to do or refrain from doing anything which affects the administering of these rules, and to enforce the prescribed penalties.

(c) Each umpire has authority to rule on any point not specifically covered in these ru les.

(d) Each umpire has authority to disqualify any player, coach, manager or substitute for objecting to decisions or for unsportsmanlike conduct or language, and to eject such disqualified person from the playing field. If an umpire disqualifies a player while a play is in progress, the disqualification shall not take effect until no further action is possible in that play.

(e) Each umpire has authority at his discretion to eject from the playing field (1) any person whose duties permit his presence on the field, such as ground crew members, ushers, photographers, newsmen, broadcasting crew members, etc., and (2) any spectator or other person not authorized to be on the playing field.

9.02 (a) Any umpire's decision which involves judgment, such as, but not limited to, whether a batted ball is fair or foul, whether a pitch is a strike or a ball, or whether a runner is safe or out, is final. No player, manager, coach or substitute shall object to any such judgment decisions.

(a) Players leaving their position in the field or on base, or managers or coaches leaving the bench or coach's box, to argue on BALLS AND STRIKES will not be permitted. They should be warned if they start for the plate to protest the call. If they continue, they will be ejected from the game.

(b) If there is reasonable doubt that any umpire's decision may be in conflict with the rules, the manager may appeal the decision and ask that a correct ruling be made. Such appeal shall be made only to the umpire who made the protested decision.

(c) If a decision is appealed, the umpire making the decision may ask another umpire for information before making a final decision. No umpire shall criticize, seek to reverse or interfere with another umpire's decision unless asked to do so by the umpire making it.

(c) The manager or the catcher may request the plate umpire to ask his partner for help on a half swing when the plate umpire calls the pitch a ball, but not when the pitch is called a strike. The manager may not complain that the umpire made an improper call, but only that he did not ask his partner for help. Field umpires must be alerted to the request from the plate umpire and quickly respond. Managers may not protest the call of a ball or strike on the pretense they are asking for information about a half swing.

Appeals on a half swing may be made only on the call of ball and when asked to appeal, the home plate umpire must refer to a base umpire for his judgment on the half swing. Should the base umpire call the pitch a strike, the strike call shall prevail.

Baserunners must be alert to the possibility that the base umpire on appeal from the plate umpire may reverse the call of a ball to the call of a strike, in which event the runner is in jeopardy of being put out by the catcher's throw. Also, a catcher must be alert in a base stealing situation if a ball call is reversed to a strike by the base umpire upon appeal from the plate umpire.

The ball is in play on appeal on a half swing.

On a half swing, if the manager comes out to argue with first or third base umpire and if after being warned he persists in arguing, he can be ejected as he is now arguing over a called ball or strike.

(d) No umpire may be replaced during a game unless he is injured or becomes ill.

9.03 (a) If there is only one umpire, he shall have complete jurisdiction in administering the rules. He may take any position on the playing field which will enable him to discharge his duties (usually behind the catcher, but sometimes behind the pitcher if there are runners).

(b) If there are two or more umpires, one shall be designated umpire-in-chief and the others field umpires.

9.04 (a) The umpire-in-chief shall stand behind the catcher. (He usually is called the plate umpire.) His duties shall be to:

(1) Take full charge of, and be responsible for, the proper conduct of the game;

(2) Call and count balls and strikes;

(3) Call and declare fair balls and fouls except those commonly called by field umpires;

(4) Make all decisions on the batter;

(5) Make all decisions except those commonly reserved for the field umpires;

(6) Decide when a game shall be forfeited;

(7) If a time limit has been set, announce the fact and the time set before the game starts;

(8) Inform the official scorer of the official batting order, and any changes in the lineups and batting order, on request; and

(9) Announce any special ground rules, at his discretion.

(b) A field umpire may take any position on the playing field he thinks best suited to make impending decisions on the bases. His duties shall be to:

(1) Make all decisions on the bases except those specifically reserved to the umpire-in-chief;

(2) Take concurrent jurisdiction with the umpire-in-chief in calling "Time," balks, illegal pitches, or defacement or discoloration of the ball by any player; and

(3) Aid the umpire-in-chief in every manner in enforcing the rules, and excepting the power to forfeit the game, shall have equal authority with the umpire-in-chief in administering and enforcing the rules and maintaining discipline.

(c) If different decisions should be made on one play by different umpires, the umpire-in-chief shall call all the umpires into consultation, with no manager or player present. After consultation, the umpire-in-chief (unless another umpire may have been designated by the league president) shall determine which decision shall prevail, based on which umpire was in the best position and which decision was most likely correct. Play shall proceed as if only the final decision had been made.

9.05 (a) The umpire shall report to the league president within twelve hours after the end of a game all violations of rules and other incidents worthy of comment, including the disqualification of any trainer, manager, coach or player, and the reasons therefor.

(b) When any trainer, manager, coach or player is disqualified for a flagrant offense such as the use of obscene or indecent language, or an assault upon an umpire, trainer, manager, coach or player, the umpire shall forward full particulars to the league president within four hours after the end of the game.

(c) After receiving the umpire's report that a trainer, manager, coach or player has been disqualified, the league president shall impose such penalty as he deems justified, and shall notify the person penalized and the manager of the club of which the penalized person is a member. If the penalty includes a fine the penalized person shall pay the amount of the fine to the league within five days after receiving notice of the fine. Failure to pay such fine within five days shall result in the offender being barred from participation in any game and from sitting on the players' bench during any game, until the fine is paid.

GENERAL INSTRUCTIONS TO UMPIRES

Umpires, on the field, should not indulge in conversation with players. Keep out of the coaching box and do not talk to the coach on duty.

Keep your uniform in good condition. Be active and alert on the field.

Be courteous, always, to club officials; avoid visiting in club offices and thoughtless familiarity with officers or employes of contesting clubs. When you enter a ball park your sole duty is to umpire a ball game as the representative of baseball.

Do not allow criticism to keep you from studying out bad situations that may lead to protested games. Carry your rule book. It is better to consult the rules and hold up the game ten minutes to decide a knotty problem than to have a game thrown out on protest and replayed.

Keep the game moving. A ball game is often helped by energetic and earnest work of the umpires.

You are the only official representative of baseball on the ball field. It is often a trying position which requires the exercise of much patience and good judgment, but do not forget that the first essential in working out of a bad situation is to keep your own temper and self-control.

You no doubt are going to make mistakes, but never attempt to "even up" after having made one. Make all decisions as you see them and forget which is the home or visiting club.

Keep your eye everlastingly on the ball while it is in play. It is more vital to know just where a fly ball fell, or a thrown ball finished up, than whether or not a runner missed a base. Do not call the plays too quickly, or turn away too fast when a fielder is throwing to complete a double play. Watch out for dropped balls after you have called a man out.

Do not come running with your arm up or down, denoting "out" or "safe." Wait until the play is completed before making any arm motion.

Each umpire team should work out a simple set of signals, so the proper umpire can always right a manifestly wrong decision when convinced he has made an error. If sure you got the play correctly, do not be stampeded by players' appeals to "ask the other man." If not sure, ask one of your associates. Do not carry this to extremes, be alert and get your own plays. But remember! The first requisite is to get decisions correctly. If in doubt don't hesitate to consult your associate. Umpire dignity is important but never as important as "being right."

A most important rule for umpires is always "BE IN POSITION TO SEE EVERY PLAY." Even though your decision may be 100% right, players still question it if they feel you were not in a spot to see the play clearly and definitely.

Finally, be courteous, impartial and firm, and so compel respect from all.

THE RULES OF SCORING

Index

10.00—The Official Scorer.

10.01 (a) The league president shall appoint an official scorer for each league championship game. The official scorer shall observe the game from a position in the press box. The scorer shall have sole authority to make all decisions involving judgment, such as whether a batter's advance to first base is the result of a hit or an error. He shall communicate such decisions to the press box and broadcasting booths by hand signals or over the press box loud-speaker system, and shall advise the public address announcer of such decisions if requested.

The Official Scorer must make all decisions concerning judgment calls within twenty-four (24) hours after a game has been officially concluded. No judgment decision shall be changed thereafter except, upon immediate application to the league president, the scorer may request a change, citing the reasons for such. In all cases, the official scorer is not permitted to make a scoring decision which is in conflict with the scoring rules.

After each game, including forfeited and called games, the scorer shall prepare a report, on a form prescribed by the league president, listing the date of the game, where it was played, the names of the competing clubs and the umpires, the full score of the game, and all records of individual players compiled according to the system specified in these Official Scoring Rules. He shall forward this report to the league office within thirty-six hours after the game ends. He shall forward the report of any suspended game within thirty-six hours after the game has been completed, or after it becomes an official game because it cannot be completed, as provided by the Official Playing Rules.

(b) (1) To achieve uniformity in keeping the records of championship games, the scorer shall conform strictly to the Official Scoring Rules. The scorer shall have authority to rule on any point not specifically covered in these rules.

(2) If the teams change sides before three men are put out, the scorer shall immediately inform the umpire of the mistake.

(3) If the game is protested or suspended, the scorer shall make a note of the exact situation at the time of the protest or suspension, including the score, the number of outs, the position of any runners, and the ball and strike count on the batter.

NOTE: It is important that a suspended game resume with exactly the same situation as existed at the time of suspension. If a protested game is ordered replayed from the point of protest, it must be resumed with exactly the situation that existed just before the protested play.

(4) The scorer shall not make any decision conflicting with the Official Playing Rules, or with an umpire's decision.

(5) The scorer shall not call the attention of the umpire or of any member of either team to the fact that a player is batting out of turn.

(c) The scorer is an official representative of the league, and is entitled to the respect and dignity of his office, and shall be accorded full protection by the league president. The scorer shall report to the president any indignity expressed by any manager, player, club employee or club officer in the course of, or as the result of, the discharge of his duties.

10.02 The official score report prescribed by the league president shall make provisions for entering the information listed below, in a form convenient for the compilation of permanent statistical records:

(a) The following records for each batter and runner:

(1) Number of times he batted, except that no time at bat shall be charged against a player when

(i) He hits a sacrifice bunt or sacrifice fly

(ii) He is awarded first base on four called balls

(iii) He is hit by a pitched ball

(iv) He is awarded first base because of interference or obstruction.

(2) Number of runs scored

(3) Number of safe hits

(4) Number of runs batted in

(5) Two-base hits

(6) Three-base hits

(7) Home runs

(8) Total bases on safe hits

(9) Stolen bases

(10) Sacrifice bunts

(11) Sacrifice flies

(12) Total number of bases on balls

(13) Separate listing of any intentional bases on balls

(14) Number of times hit by a pitched ball

(15) Number of times awarded first base for interference or obstruction

(16) Strikeouts

(b) The following records for each fielder:

(1) Number of putouts

(2) Number of assists

(3) Number of errors

(4) Number of double plays participated in

(5) Number of triple plays participated in

(c) The following records for each pitcher:

(1) Number of innings pitched.

NOTE: In computing innings pitched, count each putout as one-third of an inning. If a starting pitcher is replaced with one out in the sixth inning, credit that pitcher with 5⅓ innings. If a starting pitcher is replaced with none out in the sixth inning, credit that pitcher with 5 innings, and make the notation that he faced ——— batters in the sixth. If a relief pitcher retires two batters and is replaced, credit that pitcher with ⅔ inning pitched.

(2) Total number of batters faced

(3) Number of batters officially at bat against pitcher computed according to 10.02 (a) (1).

(4) Number of hits allowed

(5) Number of runs allowed

(6) Number of earned runs allowed

(7) Number of home runs allowed

(8) Number of sacrifice hits allowed

(9) Number of sacrifice flies allowed

(10) Total number of bases on balls allowed

(11) Separate listing of any intentional bases on balls allowed

(12) Number of batters hit by pitched balls

(13) Number of strikeouts

(14) Number of wild pitches

(15) Number of balks

(d) The following additional data:

(1) Name of the winning pitcher

(2) Name of the losing pitcher

(3) Names of the starting pitcher and the finishing pitcher for each team

(4) Name of pitcher credited with save.

(e) Number of passed balls allowed by each catcher.

(f) Names of players participating in double plays and triple plays.

EXAMPLE: Double Plays—Jones, Roberts and Smith (2). Triple Play—Jones and Smith.

(g) Number of runners left on base by each team. This total shall include all runners who get on base by any means and who do not score and are not put out. Include in this total a batter-runner whose batted ball results in another runner being retired for the third out.

(h) Names of batters who hit home runs with bases full.

(i) Names of batters who ground into force double plays and reverse force double plays.

(j) Names of runners caught stealing.

(k) Number of outs when winning run scored, if game is won in last half-inning.

(l) The score by innings for each team.

(m) Names of umpires, listed in this order: (1) plate umpire, (2) first base umpire, (3) second base umpire, (4) third base umpire.

(n) Time required to play the game, with delays for weather or light failure deducted.

10.03 (a) In compiling the official score report, the official scorer shall list each player's name and his fielding position or positions in the order in which the player batted, or would have batted if the game ends before he gets to bat.

NOTE: When a player does not exchange positions with another fielder but is merely placed in a different spot for a particular batter, do not list this as a new position.

EXAMPLES: (1) Second baseman goes to the outfield to form a four-man outfield. (2) Third baseman moves to a position between shortstop and second baseman.

(b) Any player who enters the game as a substitute batter or substitute runner, whether or not he continues in the game thereafter, shall be identified in the batting order by a special symbol which shall refer to a separate record of substitute batters and runners. Lower case letters are recommended as symbols for substitute batters, and numerals as symbols for substitute runners. The record of substitute batters shall describe what the substitute batter did.

EXAMPLES—"a-Singled for ——— in third inning; b-Flied out for ——— in sixth inning; c-Forced ——— for ——— in seventh inning; d-Grounded out for ——— in ninth inning; 1-Ran for ——— in ninth inning.

The record of substitute batters and runners shall include the name of any such substitute whose name is announced, but who is removed for a second substitute before he actually gets into the game. Such substitution shall be recorded as "e-Announced as substitute for ——— in seventh inning." Any such second substitute shall be recorded as batting or running for the first announced substitute.

HOW TO PROVE A BOX SCORE

(c) A box score is in balance (or proved) when the total of the team's times at bat, bases on balls received, hit batters, sacrifice bunts, sacrifice flies and batters awarded first base because of interference or obstruction equals the total of that team's runs, players left on base and the opposing team's putouts.

WHEN PLAYER BATS OUT OF TURN

(d) When a player bats out of turn, and is put out, and the proper batter is called out before the ball is pitched to the next batter, charge the proper batter with a time at bat and score the putout and any assists the same as if the correct batting order had been followed. If an improper batter becomes a runner and the proper batter is called out for having missed his turn at bat, charge the proper batter with a time at bat, credit the putout to the catcher, and ignore everything entering into the improper batter's safe arrival on base. If more than one batter bats out of turn in succession score all plays just as they occur, skipping the turn at bat of the player or players who first missed batting in the proper order.

CALLED AND FORFEITED GAMES

(e) (1) If a regulation game is called, include the record of all individual and team actions up to the moment the game ends, as defined in Rules 4.10 and 4.11. If it is a tie game, do not enter a winning or losing pitcher.

(2) If a regulation game is forfeited, include the record of all individual and team actions up to the time of forfeit. If the winning team by forfeit is ahead at the time of forfeit, enter as winning and losing pitchers the players who would have qualified if the game had been called at the time of forfeit. If the winning team by forfeit is behind or if the score is tied at the time of forfeit, do not enter a winning or losing pitcher. If a game is forfeited before it becomes a regulation game, include no records. Report only the fact of the forfeit.

RUNS BATTED IN

10.04 (a) Credit the batter with a run batted in for every run which reaches home base because of the batter's safe hit, sacrifice bunt, sacrifice fly, infield out or fielder's choice; or which is forced over the plate by reason of the batter becoming a runner with the bases full (on a base on balls, or an award of first base for being touched by a pitched ball, or for interference or obstruction).

(1) Credit a run batted in for the run scored by the batter who hits a home run. Credit a run batted in for each runner who is on base when the home run is hit and who scores ahead of the batter who hits the home run.

(2) Credit a run batted in for the run scored when, before two are out, an error is made on a play on which a runner from third base ordinarily would score.

(b) Do not credit a run batted in when the batter grounds into a force double play or a reverse force double play.

(c) Do not credit a run batted in when a fielder is charged with an error because he muffs a throw at first base which would have completed a force double play.

(d) Scorer's judgment must determine whether a run batted in shall be credited for a run which scores when a fielder holds the ball, or throws to a wrong base. Ordinarily, if the runner keeps going, credit a run batted in; if the runner stops and takes off again when he notices the misplay, credit the run as scored on a fielder's choice.

(e) Game-Winning RBI: The RBI that gives a Club the lead it never relinquishes.

NOTE: There does not have to be a game-winning RBI in every game and all game-winning RBIs must conform to Rule 10.04.

BASE HITS

10.05 A base hit shall be scored in the following cases:

(a) When a batter reaches first base (or any succeeding base) safely on a fair ball which settles on the ground or touches a fence before being touched by a fielder, or which clears a fence;

(b) When a batter reaches first base safely on a fair ball hit with such force, or so slowly, that any fielder attempting to make a play with it has no opportunity to do so;

NOTE: A hit shall be scored if the fielder attempting to handle the ball cannot make a play, even if such fielder deflects the ball from or cuts off another fielder who could have put out a runner.

(c) When a batter reaches first base safely on a fair ball which takes an unnatural bounce so that a fielder cannot handle it with ordinary effort, or which touches the pitcher's plate or any base (including home plate), before being touched by a fielder and bounces so that a fielder cannot handle it with ordinary effort;

(d) When a batter reaches first base safely on a fair ball which has not been touched by a fielder and which is in fair territory when it reaches the outfield unless in the scorer's judgment it could have been handled with ordinary effort;

(e) When a fair ball which has not been touched by a fielder touches a runner or an umpire. EXCEPTION: Do not score a hit when a runner is called out for having been touched by an Infield Fly;

(f) When a fielder unsuccessfully attempts to put out a preceding runner, and in the scorer's judgment the batter-runner would not have been put out at first base by ordinary effort.

NOTE: In applying the above rules, always give the batter the benefit of the doubt. A safe course to follow is to score a hit when exceptionally good fielding of a ball fails to result in a putout.

10.06 A base hit shall not be scored in the following cases:

(a) When a runner is forced out by a batted ball, or would have been forced out except for a fielding error;

(b) When the batter apparently hits safely and a runner who is forced to advance by reason of the batter becoming a runner fails to touch the first base to which he is advancing and is called out on appeal. Charge the batter with a time at bat but no hit;

(c) When the pitcher, the catcher or any infielder handles a batted ball and puts out a preceding runner who is attempting to advance one base or to return to his original base, or would have put out such runner with ordinary effort except for a fielding error. Charge the batter with a time at bat but no hit;

(d) When a fielder fails in an attempt to put out a preceding runner, and in the scorer's judgment the batter-runner could have been put out at first base.

NOTE: This shall not apply if the fielder merely looks toward or feints toward another base before attempting to make the putout at first base;

(e) When a runner is called out for interference with a fielder attempting to field a batted ball, unless in the scorer's judgment the batter-runner would have been safe had the interference not occurred.

DETERMINING VALUE OF BASE HITS

10.07 Whether a safe hit shall be scored as a one-base hit, two-base hit, three-base hit or home run when no error or putout results, shall be determined as follows:

(a) Subject to the provisions of 10.07 (b) and (c), it is a one-base hit if the batter stops at first base; it is a two-base hit if the batter stops at second base; it is a three-base hit if the batter stops at third base; it is a home run if the batter touches all bases and scores.

(b) When, with one or more runners on base, the batter advances more than one base on a safe hit and the defensive team makes an attempt to put out a preceding runner, the scorer shall determine whether the batter made a legitimate two-base hit or three-base hit, or whether he advanced beyond first base on the fielder's choice.

NOTE: Do not credit the batter with a three-base hit when a preceding runner is put out at the plate, or would have been out but for an error. Do not credit the batter with a two-base hit when a preceding runner trying to advance from first base is put out at third base, or would have been out but for an error. However, with the exception of the above, do not determine the value of base-hits by the number of bases advanced by a preceding runner. A batter may deserve a two-base hit even though a preceding runner advances one or no bases; he may deserve only a one-base hit even though he reaches second base and a preceding runner advances two bases.

EXAMPLES: (1) Runner on first, batter hits to right fielder, who throws to third base in unsuccessful attempt to put out runner. Batter takes second base. Credit batter with one-base hit. (2) Runner on second. Batter hits fair fly ball. Runner holds up to determine if ball is caught, and advances only to third base, while batter takes second. Credit batter with two-base hit. (3) Runner on third. Batter hits high fair fly. Runner takes lead, then runs back to tag up, thinking ball will be caught. Ball falls safe, but runner cannot score, although batter has reached second. Credit batter with two-base hit.

(c) When the batter attempts to make a two-base hit or a three-base hit by sliding, he must hold the last base to which he advances. If he overslides and is tagged out before getting back to the base safely, he shall be credited with only as many bases as he attained safely. If he overslides second base and is tagged out, he shall be credited with a one-base hit; if he overslides third base and is tagged out, he shall be credited with a two-base hit.

NOTE: If the batter overruns second or third base and is tagged out trying to return, he shall be credited with the last base he touched. If he runs past second base after reaching that base on his feet, attempts to return and is tagged out, he shall be credited with a two-base hit. If he runs past third base after reaching that base on his feet, attempts to return and is tagged out, he shall be credited with a three-base hit.

(d) When the batter, after making a safe hit, is called out for having failed to touch a base, the last base he reached safely shall determine if he shall be credited with a one-base hit, a two-base hit or a three-base hit. If he is called out after missing home base, he shall be credited with a three-base hit. If he is called out for missing third base, he shall be credited with a two-base hit. If he is called out for missing second base, he shall be credited with a one-base hit. If he is called out for missing first base, he shall be charged with a time at bat, but no hit.

(e) When the batter-runner is awarded two bases, three bases or a home run under the provisions of Playing Rules 7.05 or 7.06 (a), he shall be credited with a two-base hit, a three-base hit or a home run, as the case may be.

GAME-ENDING HITS

(f) Subject to the provisions of 10.07 (g), when the batter ends a game with a safe hit which drives in as many runs as are necessary to put his team in the lead, he shall be credited with only as many bases on his hit as are advanced by the runner who scores the winning run, and then only if the batter runs out his hit for as many bases as are advanced by the runner who scores the winning run.

NOTE: Apply this rule even when the batter is theoretically entitled to more bases because of being awarded an "automatic" extra base hit under various provisions of Playing Rules 6.09 and 7.05.

(g) When the batter ends a game with a home run hit out of the playing field, he and any runners on base are entitled to score.

STOLEN BASES

10.08 A stolen base shall be credited to a runner whenever he advances one base unaided by a hit, a putout, an error, a force-out, a fielder's choice, a passed ball, a wild pitch or a balk, subject to the following:

(a) When a runner starts for the next base before the pitcher delivers the ball and the pitch results in what ordinarily is scored a wild pitch or passed ball, credit the runner with a stolen base and do not charge the misplay. EXCEPTION: If, as a result of the misplay, the stealing runner advances an extra base, or another runner also advances, score the wild pitch or passed ball as well as the stolen base.

(b) When a runner is attempting to steal, and the catcher, after receiving the pitch, makes a wild throw trying to prevent the stolen base, credit a stolen base. Do not charge an error unless the wild throw permits the stealing runner to advance one or more extra bases, or permits another runner to advance, in which case credit the stolen base and charge one error to the catcher.

(c) When a runner, attempting to steal, or after being picked off base, evades being put out in a run-down play and advances to the next base without the aid of an error, credit the runner with a stolen base. If another runner also advances on the play, credit both runners with stolen bases. If a runner advances while another runner, attempting to steal, evades being put out in a run-down play and returns safely, without the aid of an error, to the base he originally occupied, credit a stolen base to the runner who advances.

(d) When a double or triple steal is attempted and one runner is thrown out before reaching and holding the base he is attempting to steal, no other runner shall be credited with a stolen base.

(e) When a runner is tagged out after oversliding a base, while attempting either to return to that base or to advance to the next base, he shall not be credited with a stolen base.

(f) When in the scorer's judgment a runner attempting to steal is safe because of a muffed throw, do not credit a stolen base. Credit an assist to the fielder who made the throw; charge an error to the fielder who muffed the throw, and charge the runner with "caught stealing."

(g) No stolen base shall be scored when a runner advances solely because of the defensive team's indifference to his advance. Score as a fielder's choice.

CAUGHT STEALING

(h) A runner shall be charged as "Caught Stealing" if he is put out, or would have been put out by errorless play when he

(1) Tries to steal.

(2) Is picked off a base and tries to advance (any move toward the next base shall be considered an attempt to advance).

(3) Overslides while stealing.

NOTE: In those instances where a pitched ball eludes the catcher and the runner is put out trying to advance, no caught stealing shall be charged. No caught stealing should be charged when a runner is awarded a base due to obstruction.

SACRIFICES

10.09 (a) Score a sacrifice bunt when, before two are out, the batter advances one or more runners with a bunt and is put out at first base, or would have been put out except for a fielding error.

(b) Score a sacrifice bunt when, before two are out, the fielders handle a bunted ball without error in an unsuccessful attempt to put out a preceding runner advancing one base. EXCEPTION: When an attempt to turn a bunt into a putout of a preceding runner fails, and in the scorer's judgment perfect play would not have put out the batter at first base, the batter shall be credited with a one-base hit and not a sacrifice.

(c) Do not score a sacrifice bunt when any runner is put out attempting to advance one base on a bunt. Charge the batter with a time at bat.

(d) Do not score a sacrifice bunt when, in the judgment of the scorer, the batter is bunting primarily for a base hit and not for the purpose of advancing a runner or runners. Charge the batter with a time a bat.

NOTE: In applying the above rule, always give the batter the benefit of the doubt.

(e) Score a sacrifice fly when, before two are out, the batter hits a fly ball or a line drive handled by an outfielder or an infielder running in the outfield which

(1) is caught, and a runner scores after the catch, or

(2) is dropped, and a runner scores, if in the scorer's judgment the runner could have scored after the catch had the fly been caught.

NOTE: Score a sacrifice fly in accordance with 10.09 (e) (2) even though another runner is forced out by reason of the batter becoming a runner.

PUTOUTS

10.10 A putout shall be credited to each fielder who (1) catches a fly ball or a line drive, whether fair or foul; (2) catches a thrown ball which puts out a batter or runner, or (3) tags a runner when the runner is off the base to which he legally is entitled.

(a) Automatic putouts shall be credited to the catcher as follows:

(1) When the batter is called out for an illegally batted ball;

(2) When the batter is called out for bunting foul for his third strike (Note exception in 10.17 (a) (4));

(3) When the batter is called out for being touched by his own batted ball;

(4) When the batter is called out for interfering with the catcher;

(5) When the batter is called out for failing to bat in his proper turn (See 10.03 (d));

(6) When the batter is called out for refusing to touch first base after receiving a base on balls;

(7) When a runner is called out for refusing to advance from third base to home with the winning run.

(b) Other automatic putouts must be credited as follows (credit no assists on these plays except as specified):

(1) When the batter is called out on an Infield Fly which is not caught, credit the putout to the fielder who the scorer believes could have made the catch;

(2) When a runner is called out for being touched by a fair ball (including an Infield Fly), credit the putout to the fielder nearest the ball;

(3) When a runner is called out for running out of line to avoid being tagged, credit the putout to the fielder whom the runner avoided;

(4) When a runner is called out for passing another runner, credit the putout to the fielder nearest the point of passing;

(5) When a runner is called out for running the bases in reverse order, credit the putout to the fielder covering the base he left in starting his reverse run;

(6) When a runner is called out for having interfered with a fielder, credit the putout to the fielder with whom the runner interfered, unless the fielder was in the act of throwing the ball when the interference occurred, in which case credit the putout to the fielder for whom the throw was intended, and credit an assist to the fielder whose throw was interfered with;

(7) When the batter-runner is called out because of interference by a preceding runner, as provided in Playing Rule 6.05 (m), credit the putout to the first baseman. If the fielder interfered with was in the act of throwing the ball, credit him with an assist, but credit only one assist on any one play under the provisions of 10.10 (b) (6) and (7).

ASSIST

10.11 An assist shall be credited to each fielder who throws or deflects a batted or thrown ball in such a way that a putout results, or would have resulted except for a subsequent error by any fielder. Only one assist and no more shall be credited to each fielder who throws or deflects the ball in a run-down play which results in a putout, or would have resulted in a putout, except for a subsequent error.

NOTE: Mere ineffective contact with the ball shall not be considered an assist. "Deflect" shall mean to slow down or change the direction of the ball and thereby effectively assist in putting out a batter or runner.

(a) Credit an assist to each fielder who throws or deflects the ball during a play which results in a runner being called out for interference, or for running out of line.

(b) Do not credit an assist to the pitcher on a strikeout. EXCEPTION: Credit an assist if the pitcher fields an uncaught third strike and makes a throw which results in a putout.

(c) Do not credit an assist to the pitcher when, as the result of a legal pitch received by the catcher, a runner is put out, as when the catcher picks a runner off base, throws out a runner trying to steal, or tags a runner trying to score.

(d) Do not credit an assist to a fielder whose wild throw permits a runner to advance, even though the runner subsequently is put out as a result of continuous play. A play which follows a misplay (whether or not it is an error) is a new play, and the fielder making any misplay shall not be credited with an assist unless he takes part in the new play.

DOUBLE PLAYS—TRIPLE PLAYS

10.12 Credit participation in the double play or triple play to each fielder who earns a putout or an assist when two or three players are put out between the time a pitch is delivered and the time the ball next becomes dead or is next in possession of the pitcher in pitching position, unless an error or misplay intervenes between putouts.

NOTE: Credit the double play or triple play also if an appeal play after the ball is in possession of the pitcher results in an additional putout.

ERRORS

10.13 An error shall be charged for each misplay (fumble, muff or wild throw) which prolongs the time at bat of a batter or which prolongs the life of a runner, or which permits a runner to advance one or more bases.

NOTE (1) Slow handling of the ball which does not involve mechanical misplay shall not be construed as an error.

NOTE (2) It is not necessary that the fielder touch the ball to be charged with an error. If a ground ball goes through a fielder's legs or a pop fly falls untouched and in the scorer's judgment the fielder could have handled the ball with ordinary effort, an error shall be charged.

NOTE (3) Mental mistakes or misjudgments are not to be scored as errors unless specifically covered in the rules.

(a) An error shall be charged against any fielder when he muffs a foul fly, to prolong the time at bat of a batter whether the batter subsequently reaches first base or is put out.

(b) An error shall be charged against any fielder when he catches a thrown ball or a ground ball in time to put out the batter-runner and fails to tag first base or the batter-runner.

(c) An error shall be charged against any fielder when he catches a thrown ball or a ground ball in time to put out any runner on a force play and fails to tag the base or the runner.

(d) (1) An error shall be charged against any fielder whose wild throw permits a runner to reach a base safely, when in the scorer's judgment a good throw would have put out the runner. EXCEPTION: No error shall be charged under this section if the wild throw is made attempting to prevent a stolen base.

(2) An error shall be charged against any fielder whose wild throw in attempting to prevent a runner's advance permits that runner or any other runner to advance one or more bases beyond the base he would have reached had the throw not been wild.

(3) An error shall be charged against any fielder whose throw takes an unnatural bounce, or touches a base or the pitcher's plate, or touches a runner, a fielder or an umpire, thereby permitting any runner to advance.

NOTE: Apply this rule even when it appears to be an injustice to a fielder whose throw was accurate. Every base advanced by a runner must be accounted for.

(4) Charge only one error on any wild throw, regardless of the number of bases advanced by one or more runners.

(e) An error shall be charged against any fielder whose failure to stop, or try to stop, an accurately thrown ball permits a runner to advance, providing there was occasion for the throw. If such throw be made to second base, the scorer shall determine whether it was the duty of the second baseman or the shortstop to stop the ball, and an error shall be charged to the negligent player.

NOTE: If in the scorer's judgment there was no occasion for the throw, an error shall be charged to the fielder who threw the ball.

(f) When an umpire awards the batter or any runner or runners one or more bases because of interference or obstruction, charge the fielder who committed the interference or obstruction with one error, no matter how many bases the batter, or runner or runners, may be advanced.

NOTE: Do not charge an error if obstruction does not change the play in the opinion of the scorer.

10.14 No error shall be charged in the following cases:

(a) No error shall be charged against the catcher when, after receiving the pitch, he makes a wild throw attempting to prevent a stolen base, unless the wild throw permits the stealing runner to advance one or more extra bases, or permits any other runner to advance one or more bases.

(b) No error shall be charged against any fielder who makes a wild throw if in the scorer's judgment the runner would not have been put out with ordinary effort by a good throw, unless such wild throw permits any runner to advance beyond the base he would have reached had the throw not been wild.

(c) No error shall be charged against any fielder when he makes a wild throw in attempting to complete a double play or triple play, unless such wild throw enables any runner to advance beyond the base he would have reached had the throw not been wild.

NOTE: When a fielder muffs a thrown ball which, if held, would have completed a double play or triple play, charge an error to the fielder who drops the ball and credit an assist to the fielder who made the throw.

(d) No error shall be charged against any fielder when, after fumbling a ground ball or dropping a fly ball, a line drive or a thrown ball, he recovers the ball in time to force out a runner at any base.

(e) No error shall be charged against any fielder who permits a foul fly to fall safe with a runner on third base before two are out, if in the scorer's judgment the fielder deliberately refuses the catch in order that the runner on third shall not score after the catch.

(f) Because the pitcher and catcher handle the ball much more than other fielders, certain misplays on pitched balls are defined in Rule 10.15 as wild pitches and passed balls. No error shall be charged when a wild pitch or passed ball is scored.

(1) No error shall be charged when the batter is awarded first base on four called balls or because he was touched by a pitched ball, or when he reaches first base as the result of a wild pitch or passed ball.

(i) When the third strike is a wild pitch, permitting the batter to reach first base, score a strikeout and a wild pitch.

(ii) When the third strike is a passed ball, permitting the batter to reach first base, score a strikeout and a passed ball.

(2) No error shall be charged when a runner or runners advance as the result of a passed ball, a wild pitch or a balk.

(i) When the fourth called ball is a wild pitch or a passed ball, and as a result (a) the batter-runner advances to a base beyond first base; (b) any runner forced to advance by the base on balls advances more than one base; or (c) any runner, not forced to advance, advances one or more bases, score the base on balls, and also the wild pitch or passed ball, as the case may be;

(ii) When the catcher recovers the ball after a wild pitch or passed ball on the third stirke, and throws out the batter-runner at first base, or tags out the batter-runner, but another runner or runners advance, score the strikeout, the putout and assists, if any, and credit the advance of the other runner or runners as having been made on the play.

WILD PITCHES—PASSED BALLS

10.15 (a) A wild pitch shall be charged when a legally delivered ball is so high, or so wide, or so low that the catcher does not stop and control the ball by ordinary effort, thereby permitting a runner or runners to advance.

(1) A wild pitch shall be charged when a legally delivered ball touches the ground before reaching home plate and is not handled by the catcher, permitting a runner or runners to advance.

(b) A catcher shall be charged with a passed ball when he fails to hold or to control a legally pitched ball which should have been held or controlled with ordinary effort, thereby permitting a runner or runners to advance.

BASES ON BALLS

10.16 (a) A base on balls shall be scored whenever a batter is awarded first base because of four balls having been pitched outside the strike zone, but when the fourth such ball touches the batter it shall be scored as a "hit batter." (See 10.18 (h) for procedure when more than one pitcher is involved in giving a base on balls. Also see 10.17 (b) relative to substitute batter who receives base on balls.)

(b) Intentional base on balls shall be scored when the pitcher makes no attempt to throw the last pitch to the batter into the strike zone but purposely throws the ball wide to the catcher outside the catcher's box.

(1) If a batter awarded a base on balls is called out for refusing to advance to first base, do not credit the base on balls. Charge a time at bat.

STRIKEOUTS

10.17 (a) A strikeout shall be scored whenever:

(1) A batter is put out by a third strike caught by the catcher;

(2) A batter is put out by a third strike not caught when there is a runner on first before two are out;

(3) A batter becomes a runner because a third strike is not caught;

(4) A batter bunts foul on third strike. EXCEPTION: If such bunt on third strike results in a foul fly caught by any fielder, do not score a strikeout. Credit the fielder who catches such foul fly with a putout.

(b) When the batter leaves the game with two strikes against him, and the substitute batter completes a strikeout, charge the strikeout and the time at bat to the first batter. If the substitute batter completes the turn at bat in any other manner, including a base on balls, score the action as having been that of the substitute batter.

EARNED RUNS

10.18 An earned run is a run for which the pitcher is held accountable. In determining earned runs, the inning should be reconstructed without the errors (which include catcher's interference) and passed balls, and the benefit of the doubt should always be given to the pitcher in determining which bases would have been reached by errorless play. For the purpose of determining earned runs, an intentional base on balls, regardless of the circumstances, shall be construed in exactly the same manner as any other base on balls.

(a) An earned run shall be charged every time a runner reaches home base by the aid of safe hits, sacrifice bunts, a sacrifice fly, stolen bases, putouts, fielder's choices, bases on balls, hit batters, balks or wild pitches (including a wild pitch on third strike which permits a batter to reach first base) before fielding chances have been offered to put out the offensive team. For the purpose of this rule, a defensive interference penalty shall be construed as a fielding chance.

(1) A wild pitch is solely the pitcher's fault, and contributes to an earned run just as a base on balls or a balk.

(b) No run shall be earned when scored by a runner who reaches first base (1) on a hit or otherwise after his time at bat is prolonged by a muffed foul fly; (2) because of interference or obstruction; or (3) because of any fielding error.

(c) No run shall be earned when scored by a runner whose life is prolonged by an error, if such runner would have been put out by errorless play.

(d) No run shall be earned when the runner's advance is aided by an error, a passed ball, or defensive interference or obstruction, if the scorer judges that the run would not have scored without the aid of such misplay.

(e) An error by a pitcher is treated exactly the same as an error by any other fielder in computing earned runs.

(f) Whenever a fielding error occurs, the pitcher shall be given the benefit of the doubt in determining to which bases any runners would have advanced had the fielding of the defensive team been errorless.

(g) When pitchers are changed during an inning, the relief pitcher shall not be charged with any run (earned or unearned) scored by a runner who was on base at the time he entered the game, nor for runs scored by any runner who reaches base on a fielder's choice which puts out a runner left on base by the preceding pitcher.

NOTE: It is the intent of this rule to charge each pitcher with the number of runners he put on base, rather than with the individual runners. When a pitcher puts runners on base, and is relieved, he shall be charged with all runs subsequently scored up to and including the number of runners he left on base when he left the game, unless such runners are put out without action by the batter, i.e., caught stealing, picked off base, or called out for interference when a batter-runner does not reach first base on the play. EXCEPTION: see example 7.

EXAMPLES: (1) P1 walks A and is relieved by P2. B grounds out, sending A to second. C flies out. D singles, scoring A. Charge run to P1.

(2) P1 walks A and is relieved by P2. B forces A at second. C grounds out, sending B to second. D singles, scoring B. Charge run to P1.

(3) P1 walks A and is relieved by P2. B singles, sending A to third. C grounds to short, and A is out at home, B going to second. D flies out. E singles, scoring B. Charge run to P1.

(4) P1 walks A and is relieved by P2. B walks. C flies out. A is picked off second. D doubles, scoring B from first. Charge run to P2.

(5) P1 walks A and is relieved by P2. P2 walks B and is relieved by P3. C forces A at third. D forces B at third. E hits home run, scoring three runs. Charge one run to P1; one run to P2, one run to P3.

(6) P1 walks A, and is relieved by P2. P2 walks B. C singles, filling the bases. D forces A at home. E singles, scoring B and C. Charge one run to P1 and one run to P2.

(7) P1 walks A, and is relieved by P2. P2 allows B to single, but A is out trying for third. B takes second on the throw. C singles, scoring B. Charge run to P2.

(h) A relief pitcher shall not be held accountable when the first batter to whom he pitches reaches first base on four called balls if such batter has a decided advantage in the ball and strike count when pitchers are changed.

(1) If, when pitchers are changed, the count is

2 balls, no strike,
2 balls, 1 strike,
3 balls, no strike,
3 balls, 1 strike,
3 balls, 2 strikes,

and the batter gets a base on balls, charge that batter and the base on balls to the preceding pitcher, not to the relief pitcher.

(2) Any other action by such batter, such as reaching base on a hit, an error, a fielder's choice, a force-out, or being touched by a pitched ball, shall cause such a batter to be charged to the relief pitcher.

NOTE: The provisions of 10.18 (h) (2) shall not be construed as affecting or conflicting with the provisions of 10.18 (g).

(3) If, when pitchers are changed, the count is

2 balls, 2 strikes,
1 ball, 2 strikes,
1 ball, 1 strike,
1 ball, no strike,
no ball, 2 strikes,
no ball, 1 strike,

charge that batter and his actions to the relief pitcher.

(i) When pitchers are changed during an inning, the relief pitcher shall not have the benefit of previous chances for outs not accepted in determining earned runs.

NOTE: It is the intent of this rule to charge relief pitchers with earned runs for which they are solely responsible. In some instances, runs charged as earned against the relief pitcher can be charged as unearned against the team.

EXAMPLES: (1) With two out, P1 walks A. B reaches base on an error. P2 relieves P1. C hits home run, scoring three runs. Charge two unearned runs to P1, one earned run to P2.

(2) With two out, P1 walks A and B and is relieved by P2. C reaches base on an error. D hits home run, scoring four runs. Charge two unearned runs to P1, two unearned runs to P2.

(3) With none out, P1 walks A. B reaches base on an error. P2 relieves P1. C hits home run, scoring three runs. D and E strike out. F reaches base on an error. G hits home run, scoring two runs. Charge two runs, one earned, to P1. Charge three runs, one earned, to P2.

WINNING AND LOSING PITCHER

10.19 (a) Credit the starting pitcher with a game won only if he has pitched at least five complete innings and his team not only is in the lead when he is replaced but remains in the lead the remainder of the game.

(b) The "must pitch five complete innings" rule in respect to the starting pitcher shall be in effect for all games of six or more innings. In a five-inning game, credit the starting pitcher with a game won only if he has pitched at least four complete innings and his team not only is in the lead when he is replaced but remains in the lead the remainder of the game.

(c) When the starting pitcher cannot be credited with the victory because of the provisions of 10.19 (a) or (b) and more than one relief pitcher is used, the victory shall be awarded on the following basis:

(1) When, during the tenure of the starting pitcher, the winning team assumes the lead and maintains it to the finish of the game, credit the victory to the relief pitcher judged by the scorer to have been the most effective;

(2) Whenever the score is tied the game becomes a new contest insofar as the winning and losing pitcher is concerned;

(3) Once the opposing team assumes the lead all pitchers who have pitched up to that point are excluded from being credited with the victory except that if the pitcher against whose pitching the opposing team gained the lead continues to pitch until his team regains the lead, which it holds to the finish of the game, that pitcher shall be the winning pitcher;

(4) The winning relief pitcher shall be the one who is the pitcher of record when his team assumes the lead and maintains it to the finish of the game. EXCEPTION: Do not credit a victory to a relief pitcher who is ineffective in a brief appearance, when a succeeding relief pitcher pitches effectively in helping his team maintain the lead. In such cases, credit the succeeding relief pitcher with the victory.

(d) When a pitcher is removed for a substitute batter or substitute runner, all runs scored by his team during the inning in which he is removed shall be credited to his benefit in determining the pitcher of record when his team assumes the lead.

(e) Regardless of how many innings the first pitcher has pitched, he shall be charged with the loss of the game if he is replaced when his team is behind in the score, or falls behind because of runs charged to him after he is replaced, and his team thereafter fails either to tie the score or gain the lead.

(f) No pitcher shall be credited with pitching a shutout unless he pitches the complete game, or unless he enters the game with none out before the opposing team has scored in the first inning, puts out the side without a run scoring and pitches all the rest of the game. When two or more pitchers combine to pitch a shutout a notation to that effect should be included in the league's official pitching records.

(g) In some non-championship games (such as the Major League All-Star Game) it is provided in advance that each pitcher shall work a stated number of innings, usually two or three. In such games it is customary to credit the victory to the pitcher of record, whether starter or reliever, when the winning team takes a lead which it maintains to the end of the game, unless such pitcher is knocked out after the winning team has a commanding lead, and the scorer believes a subsequent pitcher is entitled to credit for the victory.

SAVES FOR RELIEF PITCHERS

10.20 Credit a pitcher with a save when he meets all three of the following conditions:

(1) He is the finishing pitcher in a game won by his Club; and

(2) He is not the winning pitcher; and

(3) He qualifies under one of the following conditions:

(a) He enters the game with a lead of no more than three runs and pitches for at least one inning; or

(b) He enters the game, regardless of the count, with the potential tying run either on base, or at bat, or on deck (that is, the potential tying run is either already on base or is one of the first two batsmen he faces); or

(c) He pitches effectively for at least three innings.

No more than one save may be credited in each game.

STATISTICS

10.21 The league president shall appoint an official statistician. The statistician shall maintain a cumulative record of all the batting, fielding, running and pitching records specified in 10.02 for every player who appears in a league championship game.

The statistician shall prepare a tabulated report at the end of the season, including all individual and team records for every championship game, and shall submit this report to the league president. This report shall identify each player by his first name and surname, and shall indicate as to each batter whether he bats righthanded, lefthanded or both ways; as to each fielder and pitcher, whether he throws righthanded or lefthanded.

When a player listed in the starting lineup for the visiting club is substituted for before he plays defensively, he shall not receive credit in the defensive statistics (fielding), unless he actually plays that position during a game. All such players, however, shall be credited with one game played (in "batting statistics") as long as they are announced into the game or listed on the official lineup card.

Any games played to break a divisional tie shall be included in the statistics for that championship season.

DETERMINING PERCENTAGE RECORDS

10.22 To compute

(a) Percentage of games won and lost, divide the number of games won by the total games won and lost;

(b) Batting average, divide the total number of safe hits (not the total bases on hits) by the total times at bat, as defined in 10.02 (a);

(c) Slugging percentage, divide the total bases of all safe hits by the total times at bat, as defined in 10.02 (a);

(d) Fielding average, divide the total putouts and assists by the total of putouts, assists and errors;

(e) Pitcher's earned-run average, multiply the total earned runs charged against his pitching by 9, and divide the result by the total number of innings he pitched.

NOTE: Earned-run averages shall be calculated on the basis of total innings pitched including fractional innings. EXAMPLE: 9⅓ innings pitched and 3 earned runs is an earned-run average of 2.89 (3 ER times 9 divided by 9⅓ equals 2.89).

(f) On-base percentage, divide the total of hits, all bases on balls, and hit by pitch by the total of at bats, all bases on balls, hit by pitch and sacrifice flies.

NOTE: For the purpose of computing on-base percentage, ignore being awarded first base on interference or obstruction.

MINIMUM STANDARDS FOR INDIVIDUAL CHAMPIONSHIPS

10.23 To assure uniformity in establishing the batting, pitching and fielding championships of professional leagues, such champions shall meet the following minimum performance standards.

(a) The individual batting champion or slugging champion shall be the player with the highest batting average or slugging percentage, provided he is credited with as many or more total appearances at the plate in League Championship games as the number of games scheduled for each Club in his league that season, multiplied by 3.1 in the case of a major league player. EXCEPTION: However, if there is any player with fewer than the required number of plate appearances whose average would be the highest, if he were charged with the required number of plate appearances or official at bats, then that player shall be awarded the batting championship or slugging championship.

EXAMPLE: If a major league schedules 162 games for each Club, 502 plate appearances qualify (162 times 3.1 equals 502). If a National Association league schedules 140 games for each Club, 378 plate appearances qualify (140 times 2.7 equals 378)

Total appearances at the plate shall include official times at bat, plus bases on balls, times hit by pitcher, sacrifice hits, sacrifice flies and times awarded first base because of interference or obstruction.

(b) The individual pitching champion shall be the pitcher with the lowest earned-run average, provided that he has pitched at least as many innings as the number of games scheduled for each Club in his league that season. EXCEPTION: However, pitchers in National Association leagues shall qualify for the pitching championship by having the lowest earned-run average and having pitched at least as many innings as 80% of the number of games scheduled for each Club in his league that season.

(c) The individual fielding champions shall be the fielders with the highest fielding average at each position, provided:

(1) A catcher must have participated as a catcher in at least one-half the number of games scheduled for each Club in his league that season;

(2) An infielder or outfielder must have participated at his position in at least two-thirds of the number of games scheduled for each Club in his league that season;

(3) A pitcher must have pitched at least as many innings as the number of games scheduled for each Club in his league that season. EXCEPTION: If another pitcher has a fielding average as high or higher, and has handled more total chances in a lesser number of innings, he shall be the fielding champion.

GUIDELINES FOR CUMULATIVE PERFORMANCE RECORDS

10.24 CONSECUTIVE HITTING STREAKS.

(a) A consecutive hitting streak shall not be terminated if the plate appearance results in a base on balls, hit batsman, defensive interference or a sacrifice bunt. A sacrifice fly shall terminate the streak.

(b) CONSECUTIVE GAME HITTING STREAKS.

A consecutive game hitting streak shall not be terminated if all the player's plate appearances (one or more) result in a base on balls, hit batsman, defensive interference or a sacrifice bunt. The streak shall terminate if the player has a sacrifice fly and no hit.

The player's individual consecutive-game hitting streak shall be determined by the consecutive games in which the player appears and is not determined by his Club's games.

(c) CONSECUTIVE PLAYING STREAK.

A consecutive-game playing streak shall be extended if the player plays one-half inning on defense, or if he completes a time at bat by reaching base or being put out. A pinch-running appearance only shall not extend the streak. If a player is ejected from a game by an umpire before he can comply with the requirements of this rule, his streak shall continue.

(d) SUSPENDED GAMES.

For the purpose of this rule, all performances in the completion of a suspended game shall be considered as occurring on the original date of the game.

Learn the rules for all your favorite sports with Perigee's popular *Sports Rules in Pictures* series!

Illustrated throughout with clearly captioned, easy-to-follow drawings of actual playing situations, these handy guides to the rules of America's favorite sports are ideal for players, weekend athletes, and fans alike. For the last word on any dispute, these guides will provide the answer.

Baseball Rules in Pictures
By G. Jacobs and J. R. McCrory
This ready guide is a quick and easy way to learn baseball rules and check decisions. Nearly 200 captioned drawings cover sections on pitching, batting, baserunning, and fielding. Included is a foreword by legendary umpire Ron Luciano and the complete Official Rules of Baseball.

Official Little League Baseball ® *Rules in Pictures*
Introduction by Dr. Creighton J. Hale,
President, Little League Baseball
Incorporating more than 150 illustrations, the full text of Little League's Official Playing Rules, and all the latest rule changes, this straightforward guide is an indispensable handbook for the two million youngsters who play Little League baseball every year. Parents, coaches, managers, and umpires will find the book an essential companion on the field or in the stands.

Softball Rules in Pictures
By G. Jacobs McCrory
Revised by Michael J. Brown
Over 90 all-new drawings and a new, easy-to-follow text clarify the latest rules from the Amateur Softball Association of America in chapters on equipment, pitching, batting, and baserunning. The complete text of the rules is included along with umpire signals to help players and spectators follow the game more easily.

Football Rules in Pictures
Edited by Don Schiffer and Lud Duroska
Both stadium and armchair football fans will welcome this newly revised handbook including the latest Official National Football League Digest of Rules with its Summary of Penalties, pro, college, and high school interpretations of the game rules, and quick-reference guide to officials' signals.

Basketball Rules in Pictures
Edited by A. G. Jacobs
Profuse illustrations, captions, and text provide a complete explanation of the essential regulations of basketball, followed by a section on basic basketball play and patterns and a helpful guide to officials' signals.

Hockey Rules in Pictures
By The National Hockey League
Incorporating the complete text of the NHL Official Rules Book and the latest rule changes in use today, this handy book clearly and carefully explains goals and scoring, face-offs, high-sticking, board-checking, falling on the puck, and more. Includes a quick-reference guide to officials' signals.

Amateur Wrestling Rules in Pictures
By Michael Brown
With its hundreds of different techniques, wrestling is one of the most demanding and complicated sports to understand. With helpful stop-action illustrations and easy-to-read language, this practical guide explains wrestling's international rules, weight classes, officials' signals, boundary regulations, scoring, and much more.

Volleyball Rules in Pictures
By Michael Brown
Here is the first fully illustrated guide to America's fastest-growing sport, featuring the complete text of the Official United States Volleyball Rules as approved by the U.S. Volleyball Association, a handy guide to officials' hand signals, and over 150 line drawings and captions that explain every aspect of the game.

Golf Rules in Pictures
An Official Publication of the United States Golf Association
Introduction by Arnold Palmer
Scores of clearly captioned pictures cover golf rules from hazards, penalty strokes, and scoring to the number of clubs allowed and what to do when you accidentally hit an opponent's ball. Included is the complete text of The Rules of Golf as approved by the U.S. Golf Association and the Royal and Ancient Golf Club of St. Andrews, Scotland.

Tennis Rules and Techniques in Pictures
By Michael J. Brown
This authoritative guide explains and illustrates the rules of tennis—including doubles play—and describes the basic techniques of tennis, providing instructions on the various grips and service and advice on court tactics. The complete text of the official rules of the United States Tennis Association is included.

Ordering *Sports Rules in Pictures* is easy and convenient. Just call 1-800-631-8571 or send your order to:

The Putnam Publishing Group
390 Murray Hill Parkway, Dept. B
East Rutherford, NJ 07073
Also available at your local bookstore or wherever paperbacks are sold.

			PRICE	
			U.S.	CANADA
_____	Track and Field Rules in Pictures	399-51620	$7.95	$10.50
_____	Official Little League Baseball® Rules in Pictures	399-51531	6.95	9.25
_____	Softball Rules in Pictures	399-51356	6.95	9.25
_____	Football Rules in Pictures	399-51479	6.95	9.25
_____	Basketball Rules in Pictures	399-51590	7.95	10.50
_____	Hockey Rules in Pictures	399-51480	7.95	10.50
_____	Amateur Wrestling Rules in Pictures	399-51589	7.95	10.50
_____	Volleyball Rules in Pictures	399-51537	6.95	9.25
_____	Golf Rules in Pictures	399-51438	6.95	9.25
_____	Tennis Rules and Techniques in Pictures	399-51405	6.95	9.25

Subtotal $_____
*Postage & Handling $_____
Sales Tax $_____
(CA, NJ, NY, PA)
Total Amount Due $_____
Payable in U.S. Funds
(No cash orders accepted)

*Postage & Handling: $1.00 for 1 book, 25¢ for each additional book up to a maximum of $3.50.

Please send me the titles I've checked above. Enclosed is my:

☐ check ☐ money order

Please charge my

☐ Visa ☐ MasterCard

Card # _____ Expiration date _____

Signature as on charge card _____

Name _____

Address _____

City _____ State _____ Zip _____

Please allow six weeks for delivery. Prices subject to change without notice.